Vija Celmins
Eugenio Dittborn
Leonardo Drew
Felix Gonzalez-Torres
Rodney Graham
Ann Hamilton
Larry Johnson
Guillermo Kuitca
Jac Leirner
Brice Marden
Kerry James Marshall
Doris Salcedo
Anna Deavere Smith
Barbara Steinman
Jeff Wall
Andrea Zittel

About Place: Recent Art of the Americas

by Madeleine Grynsztejn
with an essay by Dave Hickey

The 76th American Exhibition
The Art Institute of Chicago

Contents

Lenders to the Exhibition

The Bohen Foundation
Emanuel Hoffmann Foundation, Basel
Fonds Régional d'Art Contemporain Bretagne, France
Fonds Régional d'Art Contemporain Centre, Orléans, France
Musée Départemental de Rochechouart, France
Museum für Gegenwartskunst, Basel
The Museum of Contemporary Art, Los Angeles
National Gallery of Canada, Ottawa

Airmail Paintings Inc.
Harry W. and Mary Margaret Anderson
Vija Celmins
Leonardo Drew
Felix Gonzalez-Torres
Froelich Collection, Stuttgart
Jac Leirner
Brice Marden
Kerry James Marshall
Eileen and Peter Norton, Santa Monica
Richard Prince
Private Collection, London
Private Collection, San Francisco
Andrea Rosen, New York
Doris Salcedo
Alison and Alan Schwartz
Jordi Soley, Barcelona
Barbara Steinman
Donna and Howard Stone, Chicago
Jeff Wall

Brooke Alexander, New York
Marian Goodman Gallery, New York
Sean Kelly, New York
Koplin Gallery, Santa Monica
Olga Korper Gallery, Toronto
Margo Leavin Gallery, Los Angeles
Galerie Lelong, New York
Matthew Marks Gallery, New York
McKee Gallery, New York
Galerie Nelson, Paris
Tim Nye, New York
Andrea Rosen Gallery, New York
Jack Shainman Gallery, New York
Sperone Westwater, New York

Foreword

"About Place: Recent Art of the Americas" takes as its point of departure The Art Institute of Chicago's long-established "American Exhibition," of which this is the 76th incarnation since the series began in 1888. Dedicated to bringing the most outstanding current developments in contemporary art to Chicago audiences, the "American Exhibitions" have consistently been among the most innovative, influential, and challenging exhibitions of contemporary art presented in the Midwest. They have also proved to be the primary vehicle through which the Art Institute has demonstrated its enduring commitment to contemporary art. For the current exhibition, the museum has cast its geographic net farther out, bringing together a cross-generational gathering of emerging, under-recognized, and established artists from Canada and Latin America as well as the United States. Although hemispheric in scope, this exhibition does not purport to be a comprehensive or an equally apportioned geographic overview of contemporary art. In fact, the number of artists included here has been limited to sixteen, so that each artist may be represented in some depth. Nonetheless, the range of media in this exhibition is far-ranging: in addition to painting and sculpture, "About Place" features computer-generated imagery, photography, new site-specific installations, and performance.

The exhibition's north-south axis is particularly appropriate today given the increasing economic, social, and cultural interdependence among nations. The ratification of the North American Free Trade Agreement and the recent Western Hemisphere summit meeting should provide the framework for a "Free Trade Area of the Americas" by 2005. Starting in 1995, a common market will be established among Argentina, Brazil, Paraguay, and Uruguay; meanwhile, Colombia, Mexico, and Venezuela have pledged to erase all tariffs and quotas between the three countries over the next ten years. This economic interweaving—not to mention the concurrent migration of people, images, and ideas across borders—signals a need for an exhibition that looks at the hemisphere as a whole.

"About Place" does not mark the first time that the Art Institute has looked to a hemispheric framework for an exhibition. In 1959 the noted Chicago collector and museum patron Joseph R. Shapiro organized "The United States Collects Pan American Art," an exhibition of contemporary Canadian and Latin American paintings. His prescient remarks then serve to remind us that while "styles and traditions become exhausted and change . . . . what remains is the individual artist . . . who by the expressiveness of his art, at once personal and universal, has revealed a poetic insight into the quality of human experience."

We, too, wish to emphasize that this exhibition does not concern itself so much with national identity or heritage as with artistic expression. No doubt the works in this exhibition resonate deeply with references to the artists' cultures, but they also thwart any narrow reading that would have us confine them to a purely didactic or political plane. The works represented here have been selected for being both formally and thematically accomplished. We are indebted to these artists for bringing us to a greater awareness of place.

James N. Wood
Director and President
The Art Institute of Chicago

About Place: Recent Art of the Americas

by Madeleine Grynsztejn

About Place: Recent Art of the Americas

by Madeleine Grynsztejn

These are the actual seemings that we see,
Hear, feel, and know. We feel and know them so.
. . . .
If seeming is description without place,
The spirit's universe, then a summer's day,

Even the seeming of a summer's day,
Is description without place. It is a sense

To which we refer experience, a knowledge
Incognito, the column in the desert,

On which the dove alights. Description is
Composed of a sight indifferent to the eye.
. . . .
The future is description without place,
The categorical predicate, the arc.
. . . .
Description is revelation. It is not
The thing described, nor false facsimile.

It is an artificial thing that exists,
In its own seeming, plainly visible. . .
. . . .
Thus the theory of description matters most.
It is the theory of the word for those

For whom the word is the making of the world,
The buzzing world and lisping firmament.

It is a world of words to the end of it,
In which nothing solid is its solid self.
. . . .
It matters, because everything we say
Of the past is description without place, a cast

Of the imagination, made in sound;
And because what we say of the future must portend,

Be alive with its own seemings, seeming to be
Like rubies reddened by rubies reddening.

—Wallace Stevens, "Description without Place"[1]

Introduction

I have been working... to incorporate in the manner of telling a sense of place, of not just who I am in the present but where I am coming from, the multiple voices within me. I have confronted silence, inarticulateness. When I say, then, that these works emerge from suffering, I refer to that personal struggle to name that location from which I come to voice.

—bell hooks[2]

A whole history remains to be written of spaces—which would at the same time be the history of powers (both of these terms in the plural)—from the great strategies of geopolitics to the little tactics of the habitat.

—Michel Foucault[3]

The nation, says Bloom. A nation is the same people living in the same place.... By God, then, says Ned, laughing, if that's so I'm a nation for I'm living in the same place.

—James Joyce[4]

This exhibition focuses on the work of sixteen artists from Canada, Latin America, and the United States for whom "place"—meaning the original, cultural, social, geographic, and/or political landscapes simultaneously occupied by the artist—is of paramount importance. Not a movement so much as a keenly felt sensibility, the coherent impulse of this exhibition addresses the varied nature of locale—from the actual to the remembered or imagined, from the intimate to the expansive—on an emblematic level, in the language of art. Though an ancient subject of art and literature, "place" carries a particularly acute charge today, due to the conditions of our contemporary existence in the late twentieth century.

In the western hemisphere specifically, among the most important currents within and outside of the aesthetic realm is the significant economic, social, and cultural interdependence among nations. In part caused by the constant migration of populations and the ensuing exchange of ideas and customs; the pervasive flow of the electronic media and the ease of long-distance transportation; and an economic integration by way of trade agreements and an international framework for consumer production and distribution, metropolitan centers and peripheral areas alike (though to varying degrees) are acquiring a commonality of experience and outlook.

Paradoxically, within the art world, these factors have not laid the foundation for a hemispheric synthesis. On the contrary, rather than a unified or homogenous artistic expression, the artists in this exhibition retain a highly individualized vision, primarily because they look to local experience and their specific circumstances as sources for their work. The places here envisioned are as intimate as the body (the first and most intensely known location) or the bed (a primal dwelling); and encompass "the little tactics of the habitat" (a spider's web or a person's "living unit"), the social sphere (the spaces of the city), and nature (in various degrees of domestication), extending to the outermost edges of the known world glimpsed in a starry night sky. The artists' interpretations of and viewers' responses to these made "places" are equally diverse, from positively embracing to rejecting or defying the notion of place and its attendant characteristics. The artists bring to these far-ranging evocations of location the intimate knowledge of their national origins, personal and cultural identity, and sense of place—the very issues called into question by an ongoing hemispheric redefinition that is part of a worldwide experience of deracination, circulation, and estrangement.

In fact, the emphasis on place in the work of a number of artists in this exhibition inversely points up the sense of a profound *displacement* that lends poignant weight to these works' insistence on place: whether this insistence is in the form of an affirmation of an artwork's indisputable presence and substantiality, the assertion of a (however relatively) stable identity and community (two characteristics of a definable locale), or the conviction of one's beliefs, no matter how "hybridized" or shot through with "outside" influences. The disintegration of a binding view—probably the defining factor in our late twentieth-century existence—is made manifest in our understanding of place as fragmented and discontinuous, formed from a series of disjunctive experiences that at the same time resist complete dissolution. The works in the show affirm this provisional nature of place without abandoning it entirely. Place is questioned where works exhibit only part of a presumed whole, or where their identity is grounded in the very principle of circulation, or where the notion of a fixed or independent origin, identity, or reality is challenged in the act of embracing the nomadic and transcultural. Still, though formally fragmented or fragile, emotionally vulnerable or provisionally constructed, each work fashions a "home" of a kind from personal and individual, communal, social, natural, and metaphorical strains. In their reflection of their makers' individualized practices, the artworks lend dignity to the condition of displacement, estrangement, and exile that is endemic to the Americas.

The concern with place today stems in part from topical discussions around issues of "centrality," "periphery," and "difference," terms employed in the "multicultural discourse" that is now a permanent fixture of our cultural scene. Stemming from developments contained within Modernism (as opposed to a radical rift from Modernism), and given a more specifically political slant by post-Modernist and feminist practices beginning in the late 1970s, multiculturalism has, among other things, established a healthy suspicion of strict binary oppositions including place vs. placelessness, fixed center vs. periphery or margin, unitary and authoritative vs. diverse and equally valid knowledges. Additionally, multiculturalism has forged a critical awareness of how the individual is shaped through ineffable, everyday forces that, unwittingly or not, perpetuate the prevailing "master narrative," and works towards that central authority's disempowerment. Yet the works in this exhibition are not premeditated or structured around cultural politics or theoretical notions; rather, they are the intellectually sincere and even necessary outcomes of daily, lived reality.

Place, here, is therefore the physical foundation for a series of metaphysical proposals.[5] While consistently grounded in the immediate, in lived experience and actual practice, these works are shaped to a crucial extent by metaphor. Materialized geographies combine with projections of imaginary realms to dissolve into

the willed conceptual landspaces of works of art, each a concentrated, fervent, and veracious reflection of our day-to-day lives.
Through tenacious self-knowledge and evocative rendering, an art
work that "exists/ In its own seeming, plainly visible" is formed—
a "geography" distinct from either known native or topographical
regions, and grounded in the human capacity to remap, reconstitute, transform. In giving evidence of their links with the wider
world, the works shown here demonstrate a sense of place that is
extroverted and outward-looking, as opposed to self-enclosing
and defensive.[6] Artworks are symbolic settings that bring us back
to a heightened sense of lived experience (this after a long spell
in the land of "simulacra" that characterized much of the art of the
1980s), and with that, to the possibility for individual agency,
intervention, and action.

> *I am, not dispersed, but entirely gathered together where I
> am, in this spot which is my position and where the world, because
> of the firmness of my attachment, localizes itself.*
> —*Maurice Blanchot*[7]

Notes

1. Wallace Stevens, "Description without Place," *The Collected Poems of Wallace Stevens* (New York: Vintage Books, 1982), pp. 339–46.

2. bell hooks, *Yearning: Race, Gender, and Cultural Politics* (Boston: South End Press, 1990), p. 146.

3. Michel Foucault, "The Eye of Power," preface to J. Bentham, *Le Panoptique* (Paris: Belfond); rpt. in Colin Gordon, ed., *Power/Knowledge: Selected Interviews and Other Writings 1972–1977* (Brighton, Sussex: Harvester Press, 1980), p. 149.

4. James Joyce, *Ulysses* (New York: Random House, 1946), p. 325. I owe this reference to William Anastasi.

5. Steven Holl, *Anchoring* (Princeton, N.J.: Princeton Architectural Press, 1989), p. 9.

6. This latter focus on "place" has been taken to an extreme worldwide in acts of genocide or "ethnic cleansing," driven by rabid notions of ethnicity or nationhood, and closer to home, in sectarian politics that would destroy any sense of regard for other than the overwhelmingly consensual opinion.

7. Maurice Blanchot, "Sleep, Night," in *The Space of Literature*, trans. Ann Smock (Lincoln: University of Nebraska Press, 1982), p. 265.

The Artists

The radicalism of measures to treat people as though they had never existed and to make them disappear is frequently not apparent at first glance.

—Hannah Arendt[1]

Since the mid-1980s **Doris Salcedo** has created sculptures and installations that are defiantly grounded in the horrors of everyday existence in her native Colombia. Salcedo herself willingly if critically abides within the state of constant threat characteristic of life in contemporary Colombia. She even attempts to dwell in a fellowship of suffering by staying in contact with families of the *desaparecidos* (the "disappeared") and basing her art on direct verbal reports attained from victims' relatives and friends. These reports enable her to elaborate on her self-imposed task, which is to describe, explain, redeem, and even temper the dread and the pain experienced by her community. At the heart of Salcedo's work is the projection of a space for an unacknowledged "community"—for the victims of the violence, random or deliberate, indiscriminately meted out by the military and paramilitary authorities in Colombia. Salcedo extends visibility to a hidden geography—to the secret "place" of the power structures responsible for an order of torture that is ordinarily unseen and therefore incommunicable, and that is flatly disclaimed by the authorities. She exposes, in other words, an underlying Colombian landscape of intimidation. In countries like Colombia, where the government is highly unstable, real human suffering is put at the service of groups or individuals capable of establishing their authority, however fraudulent, undemocratic, or cruel, only by means of a threat of personal injury or of "disappearance."[2] By bringing to light—by giving place and voice to—the Colombian people's hidden experiences of torture, Salcedo helps fashion a discourse in which the reality of the pain known to victims and survivors can be talked about, recognized, and legitimated. This discourse may even serve as a source of strength and closure for the damaged community, and perhaps consequently weaken the existing, but illegitimate, power structures. In this way Salcedo's project resembles that of Joseph Beuys (see fig. 1) and his idea of the artist as "social sculptor," intent on reform through the healing of personal, political, and spiritual "wounds."

Salcedo's sculptural vocabulary takes the domestic object as its point of departure (see fig. 2). Shoes, bed springs, armoires, chairs, doors are converted by dint of slow human labor into functionless, emotionally fraught objects. Often these objects will have embedded in them the impression of a particular person's body, the traces or scars of everyday use, the intimate molding of someone's feet and toes on the leather of a favorite pair of shoes. The lives of these objects as useful extensions of the human body are radically suspended by the artist, who may wrap the bed springs in gauze, partially bury or repress furniture in plaster and cement, render shoes inaccessible or doors unusable, and thus convey the sense of a home brought to an absolute standstill through some kind of brutal and unnamable intervention. Salcedo's sculptures allude by metaphorical indirection to a savage destruction of the domestic sphere that is nearly impossible to express and almost never witnessed.

Damage is done to the very surfaces or "skins" of these sculptures: abrasions, gashes, and searings that also function as formal elements. At the same time, Salcedo has brought a variety of healing labor—wrapping, grafting, sewing—usually associated with the home or the hospice, to bear on the surfaces; her sculptures thus also seemingly record acts by which a wounded thing or even a psyche is mended.

La Casa Viuda I [The Widowed House I] (fig. 3) is one of a series of sculptures in which the primary formal element is a found door. The work explicitly refers to the homes from which residents have been forcibly removed to the Colombian countryside as punishment for their political activities or for other transgressions in the eyes of paramilitary authorities. These sculptures are placed by Salcedo in passageways between rooms so that they often obstruct the normal flow of traffic. The isolation of the work through its displacement to a corridor or margin poetically and poignantly embodies the condition of "forgottenness" experienced by displaced people. The brutal juxtaposition of incongruous furniture elements within *La Casa Viuda* further recapitulates for the viewer the violence wreaked upon a habitation, upon the "space of the family,"[3] which formerly was—and ideally is—a safe haven from the vagaries, if not the barbarities, of the public sphere. Yet, in its elaborate and delicate details, this sculpture of flayed and dismembered parts reveals a kind of resistance to the violence apparently inflicted upon it. *La Casa Viuda* is guided by an almost decorative tendency, and it draws attention to a way of making, working, and ultimately surviving that is fundamentally feminine, domestic, and, in its patterns of obsessive repetition, both determinedly and consolingly ritualistic.

Atrabiliarios [Defiant] (pls. 38–41) immerses the viewer in an environment succinctly composed only of shoes inserted into wall niches. Each of these niches is closed off from the room by a semiopaque skin of dried animal bladder that has been sewn to the wall, as if the niche were a gigantic rectangular gash that had been coarsely sutured over. These niches are accompanied by a series of empty boxes made of animal fiber and placed on the floor. The niche-receptacles, which with their contents are partially buried in the wall, have a funereal character reminiscent of religious reliquaries; and indeed, Colombian cemeteries regularly contain small niches to hold the body's cremated ashes.[4] The shoes, highly personal but piecemeal remains of a loved one, in Salcedo's installation thus read as relics, as objects of mourning and remembrance,

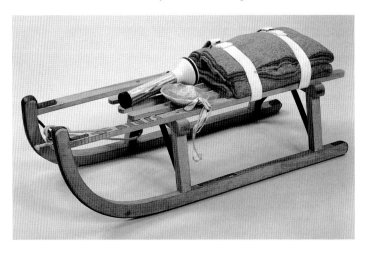

transforming *Atrabiliarios* into a commemorative site. In fact, the shoes belong to actual women who have been made to "disappear," and they were given to Salcedo by the victims' families. Salcedo brings us close to the bodily experience of pain inflicted on these unknown, nearly wholly effaced women, partly because she shows that our reality is divided from theirs by only a scrim of translucent skin—the very skin or surface that separates us from our own world and through which we are made to feel life most finely, most intensely.

Seen through the hazy layer of animal tegument, like a long-forgotten memory, the contents of each successive niche cannot be entirely denied or confirmed. The shoes appear suspended in a middle ground suggestive of the very space between life and death now occupied by their owners: a limbo within which identity is now not merely forever fixed, but also forever subject to endless erasure or dematerialization. *Atrabiliarios* is a portrait of disappearance. The whereabouts and/or deaths of these women have never been ascertained, and they are appropriately present only by proxy, by artifactual traces, by abandoned and personal effects. As death is never witnessed, mourning cannot be brought to a conclusion; in its stead grows an irresolvable sense of loss. Thus *Atrabiliarios* is not only a portrait of disappearance, but a portrait of the survivors' mental condition of wracking uncertainty, longing, and mourning. The repetition of niches extends the individual experience of each victim and her family to encompass a collective suffering. By creating a public place for the experience *and* the mourning, both of which ordinarily are private, even unspeakable, Salcedo asserts the latent powerful presence of a community of sufferers. Although displaced from their original contexts, the women's shoes retain a raw, visceral immediacy that makes urgent a tragic historical truth. By blurring them to the limits of (in)visibility, Salcedo summons the force generated by their strangely absent presence. *Atrabiliarios* insists upon the horror of fading and forgetting, and the life-or-death importance of holding onto memory. Salcedo's need to witness is part of a larger "struggle of memory against forgetting, a politicization of memory that distinguishes nostalgia, that longing for something to be as once it was, a kind of useless act, from that remembering that serves to illuminate and transform the present."[5]

Art comes so much out of a place where you trust yourself, out of the landscape you come out of.
—Ann Hamilton[6]

At its core the work of **Ann Hamilton** is driven by and shot through with the philosophy of the American heartland—its work ethic, its commitment to physical labor, its conviction of a symbiotic relationship between nature and culture. Having grown up in the suburbs of Ohio (to which she has returned to live), Hamilton is surrounded by a landscape of which the primary characteristic is its radical domestication and utilization by the human hand. The area of the United States known as the Midwest is profoundly agrarian, historically dominated both in fact and spirit by its plowed fields, barns, and woodsheds, before which the prairies and forests were long ago made to vanish. Each of Hamilton's installations is a metaphorical equivalent of the interaction between human being and nature as it has been played out in the midwestern landscape. Hamilton constructs eccentric, temporally bounded ecosystems that, during their lifespan (of days or weeks), are directly acted upon by human beings. Many of her works include a real human agent or actor, always solitary, whose role is that of a sentinel or a keeper, and who functions as one of many mutually dependent elements, animate and inanimate, organic and inorganic, in a Hamilton tableau vivant (see pls. 17–19). This individual, usually oblivious of his or her surroundings as well as of any viewers, may be absorbed in carrying out a rudimentary and repetitive task. He or she is, in fact, divorced from any real maintenance of the work, but rather bears witness to and is the human remnant of the enormous labor required for the construction of the surrounding environment.

Hamilton's often mammoth installations are the result of seemingly inconsequential tasks repeated over and over by an army of volunteers upon an overwhelming accumulation of unconventional materials. Hamilton has said that ultimately her installations should be read as "the residue of labor."[7] They begin, however, with a simple gesture performed a countless number of times. The originating gesture chosen for each installation—determined by Hamilton in the privacy of her studio, and then both externalized and multiplied ad infinitum in the installation by the artist and others—becomes the work's vehicle and its subject matter. The unheroic gestures are indicative of humble industry; they are everyday actions that normally go unnoticed: rubbing, placing, or washing, for example. In fact, to the extent that these actions are mundane, monotonous, and seemingly endless, and that they result in tidy, uncluttered, yet transitory tableaux, Hamilton's work resembles nothing so much as housekeeping. This is particularly true for installations in which the activities of washing, ironing, and cleaning are part of the work's preparation (such as when seven tons of blue uniforms are carefully folded and stacked to create a mountainous heap, or when an innumerable number of starched men's shirts are each meticulously singed at the collar with gold leaf). In these cases Hamilton pays tribute to the undervalued sphere of domestic feminine labor, taking it out of the privacy of the home into a public arena and physically amassing materials in one site in such overwhelming proportions that the herculean, not to mention sisyphean, nature of domestic work is made viscerally clear.

As important as the work itself is the temporary community that Hamilton orchestrates for the making of her pieces. Process, here, is intimately dependent upon a "collective" of volunteer laborers whose assigned occupations anachronistically echo the activities of the quilting bee, barn raising, and harvest—in other words, a community of manual laborers whose purpose is as much to forge social bonds as to generate a final product. The immense human investment necessary for a Hamilton piece lends it power and poignancy; the very walls and floors can reverberate with the sense of a felt living presence, as if the space were less an architectural enclosure and more a functioning body by which the viewer is at once disconcertingly but kindly enveloped. We are never invited into these environments by sight alone, but also by sounds, odors, and even touch. Hamilton has consistently denied both visual perception and language their traditionally dominant position in the task of interpreting the world. Instead, first-hand experience, rife

with all manner of sensory information and freely evocative of associations and memories, guides and informs each viewer's response to a particular work. Through this artist's emphasis on "what the body knows"[8] as a way for her and her collaborators to create and for us to experience her art, Hamilton's installations compel us to become aware of and thus utterly present in our bodies and in the places she creates.

As of this writing, Hamilton has selected the site for her installation—the loggia on the west side of the Art Institute's Rice Building (fig. 4)—but not its content. She will determine her subject matter slowly and intuitively, after a number of visits to the site and a prolonged rumination on its history and current condition. Her research may extend to anthropology, philosophy, poetry, and fiction as well as history, and her range of allusion eventually encompasses personal associations and recollections. Still, Hamilton's choice of the loggia may provide us with clues to her interests and direction. The loggia is a long, rather narrow gallery with tapered ends; one side is punctuated by tall windows facing out on tracks of the Illinois Central Railroad and framing a view of the city skyline

Fig. 4.
Loggia, Gallery 264, within The
Daniel F. and Ada L. Rice Building of
The Art Institute of Chicago

Fig. 5.
Ann Hamilton
suitably positioned
Performance at Franklin Furnace,
New York, 1984

beyond. The visitor who takes respite in this place is perforce recalled to the Art Institute's location and integration within the fabric of the city of Chicago. The loggia's glass walls provide an unusual readymade surface. Visually penetrable, it suggestively dissolves the walls of the narrow space; physically impermeable, it also seals off what is inside from what is outside. The windows transform the cityscape into a "picture," thus recasting the viewer in the role of a voyeur cut off from the scene without. Hamilton was immediately taken with this visual collapse of inside and outside; she has always been drawn to the complex functions of boundaries: to the ways in which borders or outlines, membranes or sheaths, not only separate but also join. She has used boundaries as conceptual devices for upsetting rather than reinforcing a binary logic and for problematizing the old dichotomies of inside/outside, human/non-human, nature/culture. Hamilton's interest in boundaries may have been stimulated in part by her early training in textiles; the artist's earliest works were constructions that served as second skins for the body—the skin being the primal boundary between the self and the world (see fig. 5). "I went from creating skins and suits for the body to treating the walls of a room as a skin."[9] For recent installations, Hamilton has consistently transformed the enclosing architecture of her chosen sites into uninterruptedly vast and "breathing" fabrics or "skins," made of materials as unexpected as 750,000 pennies, ten tons of old metal linotype, and over 2,000 pounds of horse hair.

The railroad lines and the train immediately beyond the loggia windows promise to have some degree of influence on the installation Hamilton will construct here. The literal and unusual intersection of the train and the museum inspired an earlier work by another contemporary artist. For his 1980–82 installation *Watch*

the Doors Please, the French conceptualist Daniel Buren created a "moving art work" that employed as its "canvases" the doors of railroad cars heading past the windows of The Art Institute of Chicago on their way to and from the city's southern suburbs.[10] The doors became the conveyors of Buren's signature stripes (fig. 6). Hamilton, a child of the Midwest, fully understands the historical importance of the railroad to the midcontinent and especially to the city of Chicago. During the nineteenth and early twentieth centuries, the train profoundly and irrevocably altered the landscape and economy of the Midwest: as a "powerful iron agency,"[11] it linked city with country and allowed the former fundamentally to reshape the latter by turning the frontier into urban hinterlands—forests and prairies into farms, parks, and suburbs—and the city itself into a major cosmopolitan center (i.e., "Nature's Metropolis"[12]) uniquely informed by the character of its surrounding countryside. Hamilton's works metaphorically elaborate on this intimate, reciprocal, and often ambivalent connection between city and country, nature and culture, that the train helped effect. They project a geography of compromise and exchange—never nostalgically conjuring up a lost aboriginal or Edenic nature—and acknowledge the strange and significant beauties of a landscape commingling nature with human action.

Fig. 6.
Daniel Buren (French, born 1938)
Watch the Doors Please, 1980–82
Photo/souvenir: a work in situ
and motion
The Art Institute of Chicago with
the permission of The Regional
Transportation Authority, The Illinois
Central Gulf Railroad, and the South
Suburban Mass Transit District
View from The Art Institute's Morton
Wing stairhall

As do Ann Hamilton's installations, **Rodney Graham**'s works focus on the relationship between city and country, but rework the image and perception of nature through the prism of the Romantic tradition. Graham's *Reading Machine for Lenz* (fig. 7) takes as its point of departure a novella written by Georg Büchner in 1835, in which the protagonist, Lenz, takes rapturous walks through nature while carrying on an internal (and irrational) monologue. Graham found two instances early in Büchner's text in which the phrase "through the forest" occurs; the portion of the story between these two phrases has been typeset exactly to fill five pages, and the pages in turn have been inserted into a wood-and-brass stand with a two-sided rotating panel. As the panels of this "reading machine" are turned, the story seamlessly folds back into itself at the point where the repetition occurs. Graham has thus constructed "a continuous sequence of loop-like repetitions,"[13] that short-circuits the story and condemns Lenz to being lost forever in the woods. The archetypally Romantic communion with nature has been transformed into a neurotically redundant and nightmarishly inescapable experience.

First produced in 1983 as a bound book and only recently made into a sculpture, *Reading Machine for Lenz* reflects the artistic practice of the early 1980s of "appropriation," that is, the representation of preexisting cultural products with a view to highlighting their ideological undercurrents.[14] Appropriation has consistently been Graham's modus operandi since the mid-1970s; and, whether the vehicle of exposé has been a photograph, sculpture, architectural model, drawing, or print, the artist's chief target has always been the language, visual and verbal, of the lyrical Romantic tradition. Graham has described his work as "concerned in one way or another with culturally swept-out or depopulated landscapes and images of nature construed from the perspective of Romanticism and its critique."[15] For instance, where *Reading Machine for Lenz* uses repetition, the photo series *Stanley Park Cedars, Vancouver* (pls. 15–16) uses inversion to obstruct and drain from the image its conventional Romantic meaning. The inverted images of solitary tree trunks displace the emphasis from pictured nature to the very mechanism by which the images were produced—the camera—which in recording any image always flips it upside-down. As in *Lenz*, Graham here has exposed the mechanical underpinnings of a Romantic "text" that would otherwise lull us with its narrative continuity, its seeming visual transparency, or with any other formal hallmarks of supposed truth-telling.

The particular Romantic tradition that Graham engages and would debunk has been labeled "Commonwealth Romanticism"[16] by his colleague Jeff Wall. "Commonwealth Romanticism" as perceived by Wall is an aesthetic that took root during the British colonial era, and that centers upon an almost pantheistic rapport with the "sublime" natural landscape of the west coast of British Columbia. This aesthetic has informed much of western Canadian art-making, both as a source of uncontested ideas and conceits and as matter for critical counterpoint. Pivotal to the development of Commonwealth Romanticism is the work of Emily Carr, whose highly subjective, expressionistic paintings of forest landscapes undercut the salient Romantic tradition by introducing an element of protest and disquiet in the form of images of blasted tree trunks and solitary trees left in a waste of devastation. Carr's work, while firmly

[It is a] model of our real relation to parklands and nature reserves; it recognized them as stage-sets, isolated objects of alienated contemplation. The work built upon its audiences the growing awareness of environmental abuse to make perceptible the neurotic aestheticism inherent in the contemplation of special parts of nature dissociated from the labouring totality. Ravine *explicitly staged this isolation of nature and spectators from each other, and made the experience of a "special place" one of anxiety and guilt rather than absorptive repose.*[19]

Graham's *Millennial Project for an Urban Plaza (with Cappuccino Bar)* (pl. 14) is a maquette for a fanciful and eccentric piece of architecture intended to house a gigantic pin-hole camera. An elaborate tower structure, *Millenial Project* is designed to be placed in an open plaza at some distance from the spot where, at the time of the tower's construction, an oak seedling is to be planted. The location of the tower relative to the seedling is such that the camera's gargantuan fixed eye will eventually (after many years) be occupied by the image of the tree that will have slowly, inexorably, grown up. This image, projected onto an immense interior screen, will hover—like Graham's inverted photos of the cedar trunks—upside-down; until the tree has reached the necessary height, however, the screen will show merely a void of sky (see fig. 9). In this whimsical project, Graham has devised a way to reverse the traditional urban-rural hierarchy in which trees serve only the city's interests, as a type of "street furniture," raw resource for economic gain, and building material. Here Graham "commits a building to the task of waiting patiently for a tree to grow and then, when it is grown, to preserve it in its sight."[20] In this way the tree makes a dramatic (re)appearance, in no way tied to its potential utility, in the city where thrive those bureaucracies that have managed its destruction. The (re)appearance, though, is only of a phantom kind—an image in a camera obscura that is always reversed, partly out of focus, and trapped by the circumstance of a mechanical reproduction.

entrenched in the lyrical-romantic tradition, was the first to point to the violence done by the then-nascent Canadian logging industry to the native forest and to its First Nation inhabitants. In paintings such as the classic *Scorned as Timber, Beloved of the Sky* (1935; fig. 8), Carr conveyed a searing criticism of the activities and the advancement-at-all-cost of unbridled industrialism.

Graham continues Carr's legacy and practice of undermining the Romantic aesthetic by critically readapting or restructuring its visual cues.[17] Where in Carr's paintings a single tree may stand as lonely witness to a surrounding field of annihilation, in Graham's photographs the focus has been deliberately contracted to a solitary truncated tree trunk similarly indicative of an outside destructive force. It is significant that Graham has chosen as his subjects first-growth cedar trees located in a modern park in the city of Vancouver: for the park itself is both a consequence and a kind of substitutive camouflage of the wholesale loss of the primeval British Columbian forests. Historically, parks and forest preserves were created only in the wake of aggressive economic expansion, and in response to a slowly dawning awareness of the disappearance of native ecology. Parks do not merely protect the small bit of nature they enclose, but they also conceal the effects of development (like clearing and logging) by projecting the chimerical picture of an intact Romantic landscape. Indeed, the "provision of parks and protected wilderness areas, large in themselves though only a minute percentage of the province's land area, ensures that the wilderness sojourner will rarely, if ever, come face to face with [the] violence"[18] of deforestation. Graham, by narrowing his photographs' focus to a tree trunk, relates the cedar less to its wild ancestor than to its tamed and isolated counterpart in the city: to the straight, columnlike tree trained up to embellish the boulevard. Graham's suite of photographs, for all their beguiling naturalistic detail, only highlight the alienation from nature of the trees and of ourselves. Jeff Wall's description of an earlier Graham project titled *Ravine* is applicable:

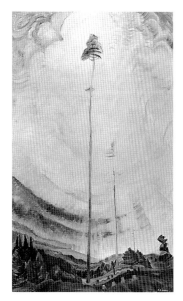

Fig. 7.
Rodney Graham
Reading Machine for Lenz, 1983/93
Printed paper, glass, Plexiglas, stainless steel, and wood
21¾ x 23½ x 7¾ inches at base
(55.2 x 59.7 x 19.7 cm)
Edition 1/3
Private Collection, London

Fig. 8.
Emily Carr (Canadian, 1871–1945)
*Scorned as Timber,
Beloved of the Sky,* 1935
Oil on canvas
44 x 27 inches (112 x 68.9 cm)
Vancouver Art Gallery, Emily Carr Trust

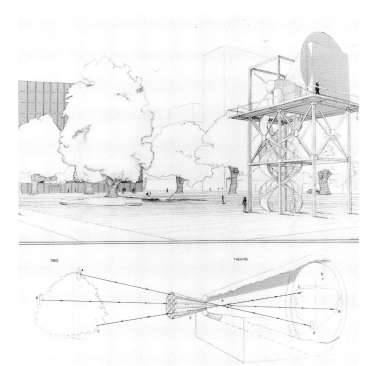

Graham's art, at once critical and utopian, playful and pointed, emphasizes the specific ways in which we contemplate, render, preserve, destroy, and take responsibility for nature through technology. With the *Millenial Project*, Graham suggests a new type of urban architecture and geography capable of reconciling not only city and country, but also the city to its past treatment of nature. This future metropolis, made responsive to environmental, political, economic, and cultural challenges, would no longer conceal but rather spotlight those contradictory forces—among them the catastrophic injury to nature—that have aided in its development. The citizens of this future place would no longer be allowed the false consolations of the forest-park, but would be required to acknowledge their alienation from any arcadia. In place of a real Arcadia, however, they will have built a city of imaginative architectural détente, "an urban fantasy of the picturesque brought into city central."[21]

Fig. 9.
Rodney Graham
Millenial Project for an Urban Plaza,
1986 (rendering of installation)
Pencil on mylar
22³/₁₆ x 22 inches
(56.4 x 56.3 cm)
Vancouver Art Gallery

Think of being able to own your own home and being able to bring it along wherever you go....Think of being able to create a small nucleus designed to perfectly accommodate just your needs....a nucleus that has the ability to remain constant even when surroundings are ever changing....The A–Z 1993 Unit unfolds to create a series of "rooms" which may be personalized to satisfy your particular needs.

—Andrea Zittel[22]

The comforts of home take on an entirely new meaning in the work of **Andrea Zittel**. Zittel creates what she calls "perfect units"— "prototypes to cleanse, feed, and comfort the human body"[23]— each of which is comprised of a rectangular box capable of unfolding into several contiguous cells that together contain everything one needs to live easily, efficiently, and economically: a bed space, a kitchen, an office, closets, and cupboards. Intended to function as a portable capsule of security and comfort, the perfect unit can be customized to suit each purchaser's needs and specifications (see pls. 55–58). In both her exhibitions and the printed material designed to accompany them, Zittel makes a conscious nod to the furniture showroom; and she unashamedly attempts to seduce the viewer—a potential consumer—with the language as well as the look, or the visual ruses, of advertising (see pl. 54). Such a conflation, however qualified, of art gallery and furnishings boutique has an antecedent in the work of Pop artist Claes Oldenburg, whose *Bedroom Ensemble* (see fig. 10) not only collapsed public and private, "high" and "low" spaces, but also pointed up the functional identity between gallery and showroom as spaces alike for commercial display and marketing. For "About Place," Zittel will exhibit units that have already been lived in: she believes that, while galleries and showrooms are the launching-grounds for brand-new objects, museums exist to preserve and re-present things that have already circulated in the world.

In their isolation, self-sufficiency, and standardization, as well as their promise of private ownership and their concomitant atomization of community, Zittel's perfect units are eccentric second cousins to the postwar suburban home, and, by extension, to the suburban housing development. Zittel's peculiar revisiting of the conventional home design ties her work to that of Dan Graham, an astute observer of the American suburbs whose own utopian projects—combining conceptual art and architecture—lay bare the ideological underpinnings of everyday life.[24] Graham's well-known article *cum* art project "Homes for America" (fig. 11) analyzes and deconstructs tract house developments as but one manifestation of the larger social forces at work on the American landscape. His description of the standardized, prefabricated, mass-produced houses built in the "California Method" might be applied to Zittel's living units; and it is perhaps of no little significance that Zittel was raised and went to college in San Diego:

Each house in a development is a lightly constructed "shell".... Shells can be added or subtracted easily. The standard unit is a box or a series of boxes.... Developments stand in an altered relationship to their environment.... the houses needn't adapt to or attempt to withstand nature. There is no organic unity connecting the land site and the home. Both are without roots— separate parts in a larger, pre-determined, synthetic order.[25]

As Graham also points out in "Homes for America," the suburban residential development allows a limited type of individual home modification by the homeowner, who may, for example, express him- or herself in the selection of outdoor paint color. "Under such circumstances, which typify consumer capitalism everywhere, the means for self-expression are radically reduced. But they are not eliminated."[26] Similarly, Zittel offers her clients a restricted range of variations on the basic structure of her perfect units. And it is Zittel's stated (tongue-in-cheek?) hope that her product, like the model home of the suburban development, will eventually be mass-produced and thereby become a universally accessible means to "the better life."

It may have also been through California's suburban architecture that Zittel initially, if unwittingly, came into contact with the Modernist ideas, however bastardized or diluted, that have since informed her artistic output.[27] Her living units, though deliberately awkward in construction and humble in their materials (such as plywood), compositionally adhere to the Modernist idiom: a stripped-down language of elemental geometric shapes in which form is dictated solely by materials, by construction methods, and by ultimate function. Decoration, in and of itself, has been largely banished. Zittel, however, has not only borrowed Modernism's reductive aesthetic, but also adopted its moral dimension; in the spirit of early twentieth-century Russian Constructivism, the Bauhaus academy, and the De Stijl movement, Zittel designs little "buildings" intended to improve—to simplify and thus purify—the lives of the individuals who inhabit them. Zittel's perfect units will in turn perfect *us* by reforming or reinforcing our behavior to sympathetically reflect a structurally disciplined environment. Under the label "A–Z Administrative Services" (the title she has given to her project for mass-producing the entire range of her work), Zittel "is dedicated to the endeavor of creating new structures to perfect the organization of a life. These structures, while dictatorial in one dimension, are liberating in another."[28] Indeed, these furniture-formations embody a vision of a way of life that fantastically oscillates between a simple, Shaker-like austerity and a fascistic overdetermination. In this installation of *used* living modules, however, Zittel relinquishes absolute authoritative design and welcomes the unexpected vagaries and felicities of coauthorship.

If the domestic realm is considered a metaphor for the culture at large, then Zittel's dwellings reveal our cultural biases and tendencies most pointedly and poetically. Her units, all single-person habitats, may be seen as symptomatic of the dissolution of the nuclear family, and of the family home, in our society. The citizens of Zittel's revolutionary one-person households have very likely witnessed the painful disintegration of the social relationships that once

Fig. 10.
Claes Oldenburg (American, born Sweden, 1929)
Bedroom Ensemble Replica I, 1969
Environment with mixed media
119 1/3 x 201 1/2 x 255 inches
(303 x 512 x 648 cm)
Museum für Moderne Kunst, Frankfurt am Main; Former Karl Ströher Collection, Darmstadt

Fig. 11.
Dan Graham (American, born 1942)
Homes for America, 1966/67
Lithograph
Nova Scotia College of Art and Design

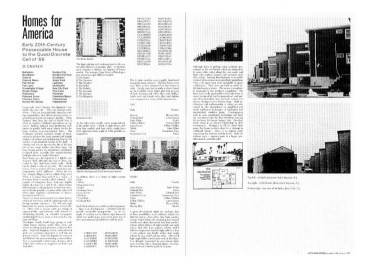

made for domesticity, and if their new living modules announce the demise of the traditional family unit, they also physically absolutely preclude its revival or even continuation. Yet Zittel's new living units do fulfill the need for a home, a sanctuary, and a place of refuge: "even in a hostile surrounding," Zittel promises us "a perfected unit in which to live,"[29] one attuned to the individual occupant's autonomy and hyper-mobility. That Zittel's units are small, collapsible and easily transported—each one "a cross between a piece of furniture and a mobile home or a suitcase"[30]—positively embraces the rootless and nomadic nature of contemporary life. The living modules, which when folded up look like nothing so much as steamer trunks or cargo crates, answer what their artist perceives as the need for a new kind of endlessly relocatable architecture with its own, internally generated sense of place—an architecture that acknowledges current "patterns of movement and settlement and work."[31] Her dwelling-forms, defiantly private, sturdily self-reliant, and readily movable, make a place that at once reflects and resists the larger cultural and social landscape of broken ties and relationships.

For the past decade, the job of the Airmail Paintings has been to come in and out of the house—the city—to...unfold and display...and then to leave, undetected...letters sent to keep distance intact.

—Eugenio Dittborn[32]

Eugenio Dittborn's works, which he calls Airmail Paintings, both span and preserve the international distances between Chile and the countless other countries to which the pieces have traveled since 1983. They do so primarily by making their itineraries a principal component of their presentation. Written on the cardboard airmail envelopes in which the Airmail Paintings are circulated, these itineraries record each work's original point of departure (the artist's home in Santiago, Chile) and the destinations of all its appointed journeys. The itineraries, which Dittborn exhibits alongside the Airmail Paintings to which they belong, are records of both endless excursions—endless migrations—and an equally endless recall to home.

Devised in part as a pragmatic response to Santiago's location on the art world's periphery, the Airmail Paintings are in format and materials inexpensive, lightweight, modestly scaled, and easy to transport; as such, they are capable of bypassing Chile's bureaucratic infrastructure (or lack thereof). Significantly, Dittborn's art and working methods were developed under and continue to bear witness to conditions enforced in Chile by General Augusto Pinochet's military dictatorship following his seizure of power in 1973 from Salvador Allende's elected Communist government. No regime in Chilean history has been more brutally repressive of divergent views. Having long lived under the weight of tyranny, Dittborn has, not unexpectedly, gravitated to an art practice that pivots upon sociopolitical issues. His pieces, furthermore, evince a powerful aversion to dogma—more specifically to the coercive forms of address and modes of persuasion typical of authoritarian regimes. While political in bent, Dittborn's works never bluntly direct either the viewer's thoughts or eventual actions, but instead generate a dialogue between an array of diverse images that is elegantly and

obliquely evocative and always barbed.

Dittborn's Airmail Paintings are repositories for vulnerable, transient images that have either been forgotten or deliberately suppressed by the official culture (whether Pinochet's military dictatorship or, much earlier, Spanish colonial rule). The recovery of these images, a subtly political act, is intended to counter the insidious erasure of people and ideas antipathetic to the dominant power: we can thus see, restored in the Airmail Paintings, Native Americans, political dissidents, petty thieves, the insane. Dittborn has remarked that his Airmail Paintings are "a way of salvaging my previous work, which was threatened, like every other cultural production in Chile in these last years, with oblivion. Power in our country constructs a social, political and cultural space which is characterized by a monstrous capacity to empty and exclude any possibility of memory. My artistic work puts itself forward, in its travels, as a little model of a possible memory."[33]

For this exhibition, Dittborn has produced a new work based on Georges Seurat's *A Sunday on La Grande Jatte—1884*, in the Art Institute's collection (see pls. 6–7). In *Airmail Painting No. 95: The 13th History of the Human Face (The Portals of H.)* (pls. 4–5), Dittborn reproduces a drawing of a funerary bundle containing the body of a man who had once served as leader of the ancient Paracas civilization (fig. 12); the body had been recovered from a second-century necropolis located in the Paracas peninsula of Peru. Dittborn's persistent concern with the recovery of individuals through literal or metaphorical exhumation, through rediscovered photographic records, or through some other form of preserved portraiture, may be attributed to the traumatic events of recent Chilean history, during which many people were made to "disappear"—some of whose bodies have only lately been unearthed in Chile's Tarapaca desert. This particular image of an ancient funerary bundle or basket undoubtedly attracted Dittborn because of the visual and functional resemblance of the bundle to the Airmail Painting. Both envelope and basket are parcels composed of layers of plain cloth that provide their contents a secure if not necessarily final resting-spot; both serve not only as places of (relative) preservation, but also as the means to a renewed "life" of restored currency and circulation.

Dittborn's further choice for this work of a detail from the Flemish Renaissance painting *Dulle Griet [Mad Meg]* by Pieter Bruegel the Elder (fig. 13) becomes strikingly appropriate when one reads in the itinerary that the Airmail Painting's first journey was to Antwerp in 1991. Dulle Griet, a symbol of human folly (she is seen emerging from the mouth of Hell laden with loot) is transformed into a far more poignantly bereft figure by the reproductions of drawings by schizophrenics with which Dittborn surrounds her (the drawings were all made by residents of a Santiago psychiatric hospital).[34] Also incorporated here are the photographed faces of men and women from the Alakawulup, Selknam, and Yamana Indian tribes—people as peripheral to and unintegrated within Chilean society as the mad—that resided at Chile's southernmost polar tip; these tribal peoples were photographed on the verge of their extinction in the 1920s by the German Catholic priest and anthropologist Martin Gusinde. Juxtaposed with the images of Dulle Griet and the Native Americans are mug shots from the 1940s of

of calm water—a suitable place to settle a

of the settlement can now be seen, unfortun

become an immense burial ground. Indeed

to define the Paraca civilisation by a

small-time Chilean criminals—petty thieves and prostitutes who were probably impoverished peasants newly immigrated to the Santiago capital. The mug shots were culled by Dittborn from a magazine, *El Detective*, published by the Chilean civil police from 1920 to 1950 and distributed to each police officer, along with his salary, at the end of every month. The variegated "gallery of marginal figures" that crowds the surface of *Airmail Painting No. 95*— "muggers, petty thieves and swindlers, pickpockets, victims, aborigines"[35]—is marshalled by Dittborn to point out the often violent consequences of the encounter between indigenous and colonizing populations, an encounter deeply inscribed in Latin American history and consciousness.

Two images, one of a raft and one of an armadillo, complete Dittborn's collage. The raft, a vehicle of exile and of return, has been lifted from a children's book that offers instructions for building toys out of commonplace or left-over materials, and thus it tacitly addresses the poverty experienced as "a constituent feature of [Chile's] national life."[36] Dittborn's work, however, conveys this poverty not only through its imagery, but also through formal devices, like choice and arrangement of materials. The cloth Dittborn employs for his Airmail Paintings' supports, to which the artist loosely stitches additional patches of frail, nonwoven material, is a cheap fabric normally used to line clothing. By means of these cloth supports, fragility, precariousness, and impermanence are physically as well as figuratively embodied in Dittborn's art—qualities made all the more vivid for us by our awareness that each Airmail Painting is repeatedly consigned to the uncertain care of the international airmail system. Yet Dittborn's works also convey a

sturdy optimism—hence the image of the armadillo, a tough-skinned South American animal whose modest size, like that of a wrapped Airmail Painting, belies its endurance, strength, and potential impact. Looking at Dittborn's work, the viewer finds his or her eye traveling from the flat of the fabric to traces of folds—marks of the Airmail Painting's being folded for insertion into its envelope or protective wrapper—and finds by the same token his or her *mind* traveling to the journey(s) Dittborn has determined the artwork must undertake.[37] For every Airmail Painting, journeying as exodus or migration is the inescapable flip-side of "locality, habitation, domestication"[38]; and each of these two opposed but reciprocally defining terms offers the only way through which its opposite can be redeemed.

The work of **Jac Leirner** provides a home for objects ordinarily assigned to a life of constant flux. Leirner's entire oeuvre is founded on the premise of finding a permanent place for materials "that ceased to have a designated location . . . in the world until her works provided a 'terminal position' [the artist's words] for them."[39] In all cases the off-beat materials from which Leirner constructs her sculpture-installations are explicitly rootless, anonymous, mass-produced things designed narrowly for the purpose of facilitating exchange or expediting travel. Money (in the form of paper currency) and airline paraphernalia (e.g., cutlery, luggage tags, air sickness bags, blankets, pillows, armchair ashtrays) belong by their very nature to no one person or place but are rather the very instruments of never-ending circulation and redistribution. The subject matter as well as the raw ingredients of Leirner's art, these materials find their original *raison d'être* hauntingly brought to an abrupt and absolute standstill within the context of each piece. Leirner wrests things out of the existing systems of circulation by which they are defined. By doing so, she does not merely expose her materials' intrinsic uselessness or vacancy, but she also readapts them to another "system," another structure, capable of endowing them with real (as opposed to phantom) meaning; out of vagrant and even distasteful material, Leirner makes assertively fixed works of art.

Though Leirner's materials are utterly commonplace, the artist's collecting of them is extraordinary: they may be hoarded, borrowed, purchased, filched, and/or received as gifts over a period of several years, until Leirner has accumulated a mass large enough for a sizable sculpture. Once gathered, her materials are subject to an equally painstaking assembly process often belied by the apparent litheness of the resulting sculptures' forms and by Leirner's own conceptual adroitness. Her working method involves the classifying, assembling, stacking, or aligning, threading, and sewing of individual elements—a method that does not so much transform these elements as reconfigure and recontextualize them. Selected for their physical properties as well as for their original "homelessness," the materials are left essentially unaltered. For example, *Todos os Cem [All the One Hundreds]*, a supple, space-devouring floor piece that undulates serpentlike across the gallery floor, is the result of three years of collecting followed by the sewing and threading of roughly 80,000 outdated Brazilian banknotes. The notes are of two kinds, a newer cruzado currency called *novo cruzado*, and an older type of bill in three different forms (*cruzeiros*,

Fig. 12. (Previous page)
Eugenio Dittborn
Airmail Painting No. 95: The 13th History of the Human Face [The Portals of H.], 1991 (detail)
Paint, stitching, and photosilkscreen on 6 sections of nonwoven fabric
Dimensions vary with installation
Courtesy Airmail Paintings Inc.

Fig. 13.
Pieter Bruegel the Elder (Flemish, c. 1525–1569)
Dulle Griet [Mad Meg], 1562?
Oil on panel
46¼ x 63¾ inches (117.4 x 162 cm)
Museum Mayer van den Bergh, Antwerp

cruzados, and *novo cruzados*), both in denominations of 100 and 100,000. Leirner has arranged all these bills by color, grading them from a light to a dark, gouachelike gray, which reflects the extent to which the money has been handled (the darker bills being well-thumbed, the palest being brand-new and unused). In Leirner's hands, a thing as physically spare as a paper banknote has been readapted to assume great literal and figurative weight, even though—or rather because—it has been neatly divorced from its original function.

The expressiveness of this sculpture is still closely tied to the connotative power of the banknotes as instruments of economic (and thus also social) transactions. It is significant that *Todos os Cem* relates to an earlier series of works called *Os Cem [The One Hundreds]* (1985–87; pls. 28–29), also produced from Brazilian currencies. By the time Leirner began exhibiting *Os Cem* in 1987, the cruzeiros that comprised her sculptures had already gone out of circulation. Rendered worthless through hyperinflation, the cruzeiros were replaced by the government with the cruzados. *Os Cem* therefore hints at the unstable and what was then the rapidly eroding state of Brazil's financial structure, a state to which the series' title, a telling pun, also alludes; the double meaning of this title would be readily understood by any Portuguese-speaking person: the "cem" in *Os Cem* means "hundred," but phonetically it is identical to the Portuguese word "sem," meaning "without." Sensitive to economic realities and to their wide-ranging social repercussions, Leirner has thus signaled in the titles of her sculptures that perverse and paradoxical conflation of a surplus excess with severe impoverishment characteristic of the Brazilian economy in the mid-1980s. In *Todos*

os Cem we are presented with nothing more nor less than an endless snaking file of worthless cold hard cash.

To live in a country where the ultimate symbol of secular value—the banknote—is continually subject to drastic revaluation, even to the bankruptcy of its meaning, is to wonder, as Leirner does, whether any bearings can ever be taken for real. It is rather as if Brazil, for its citizens, "is a fictional country. Its values are not real. Morality is absent, inverted. That's why I crave so much for the real."[40] When the economic terms by which one lives are shifted as often as three times in a single year—a situation so volatile that cruzeiro banknotes at one point bore the adjective "real" to distinguish them from their worthless predecessors—maintaining a sense of reality requires a conscious and exacting effort. It is perhaps the very disconcerting shiftlessness or fragility of Brazil's economic and social relations (a shiftlessness and fragility characteristic of many so-called developing countries) that Jac Leirner would counter with her supple yet obdurate sculptures.[41]

In a number of earlier twentieth-century artworks, the symbol of money, or money itself, has served as the predominant image and/or constitutive visual element; Marcel Duchamp's *Monte Carlo Bond* (1924; fig. 14)[42] and Andy Warhol's silkscreen paintings of dollar bills (1962) are two well-known examples.[43] Duchamp's art as a whole, both in the artist's critically tongue-in-cheek choice of materials and in his sharp questioning of established (aesthetic) values, can be considered a strong influence on Leirner's sculptures. Duchamp's perhaps most important and maverick contribution was to render a common object "precious" simply by lifting it out of its habitual context and inserting it into the space of art—a "ready-

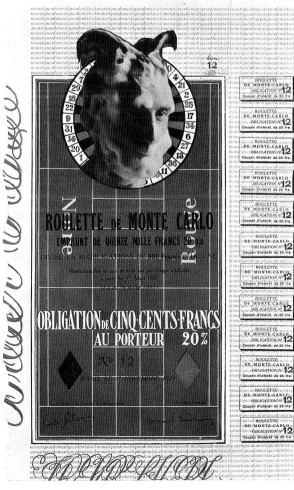

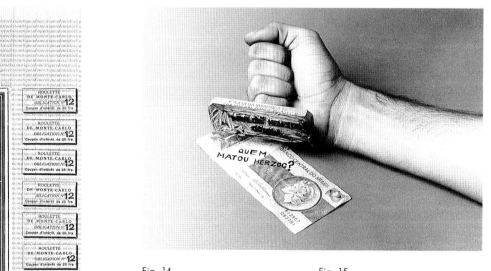

Fig. 14.
Marcel Duchamp (American, born France, 1887–1968)
Monte Carlo Bond, 1924
Photocollage on colored lithograph
12¼ x 7¾ inches (31.1 x 19.7 cm)
The Museum of Modern Art, New York, Gift of the artist

Fig. 15.
Cildo Meireles (Brazilian, born 1948)
Insertions into Ideological Circuits: The Banknote Project, 1970
Stamp on banknotes

made" artwork rendering in one succinct stroke the ephemeral permanent, the ubiquitous scarce, and the worthless valuable. Yet Leirner's work, unlike Duchamp's, relies in no significant way on accident or chance, either for the discovery of its "found" materials or for the possible ways in which they might be arranged or assembled. It is, rather, the Brazilian conceptual artist Cildo Meireles who has perhaps provided Leirner with her most important and immediate model. Between 1970 and 1975, a period in recent Brazilian history of intensely repressive dictatorship, Meireles devised his *Insertions into Ideological Circuits* project (see fig. 15), a work for which the artist stamped hundreds of banal objects like Coca-Cola bottles or cruzeiro bills with messages of social protest before releasing them back into public circulation. In this way Meireles not only attempted to subvert a blind commercial "circuit" or system, but also to circumvent the usual means of communication then being closely monitored by the military regime in power. Meireles, in a one-person guerrilla-type ideological skirmish, surreptitiously mass-distributed such incendiary questions as "Who Killed Herzog?" throughout all levels of Brazilian society.[44] Leirner's own banknote works both invoke and pay homage to Meireles's *Insertions* project.

Leirner's construction of sculptures that "seize and hold space,"[45] through the serial arrangement of almost identical constituent units, recalls Minimalist art practices, which in Brazil find a formal parallel in Concretism. Yet Leirner's collecting and classifying of objects is seemingly so compulsive in nature, and the sheer quantity of her assembled materials so unthinkably enormous, that both verge on the irrational. If her works partake on the one hand of Minimalism's pragmatic insistence on physical immediacy, they are also profoundly flavored on the other by that unique South American variation upon Surrealism that helped engender the literary work of a Gabriel García Márquez or a Jorge Luis Borges. With each of Leirner's sculptures we are made to sense the existence of a surrounding medium or environment in which a labyrinthian psy-

chology blends indistinguishably into bureaucracy, and both have flowered out of control. The influence of Minimal and Conceptual art upon Leirner's work is tempered by other sources that include a laudible Brazilian tradition developed in the sculptures and projects of Waltércio Caldas, Meireles, José Resende, Mira Schendel, Tunga, Volpi, and the Neo-Concretists Lygia Clark and Hélio Oiticica.[46] The Neo-Concretists retained Concretism's emphasis on the physical properties of the work of art—size, shape, color, a simple compositional structure—while modifying its geometric vocabulary through not only individual expressiveness but also the introduction of an interactive and transient dimension.[47] Leirner has cogently synthesized this complex legacy and gone on to develop her own quietly reductive and touchingly vulnerable work.

A sense of bodily precariousness is conveyed by the works in Leirner's more recent series, *Corpus Delicti*, and especially by a floating columnar sculpture made of airplane cutlery provisionally strung together with transparent cord (pls. 30–31). This sculpture, which Leirner suspends vertically from the ceiling, recalls an endless, bristlingly exposed but sinuous spine, having for its "vertebrae" individual knives, forks, and spoons. Each constituent part blatantly testifies to the little crime of theft by which it was taken out of its everyday world of international air space and into Leirner's art. On countless work-related journeys between 1987 and 1992, Leirner took from the airplanes in which she traveled not only cutlery, but also toiletry kits, napkins, boarding passes, blankets, and pillows for her *Corpus Delicti* works. Meaning literally "body of the crime," *Corpus Delicti* is a Latin juridical term given to the material evidence gathered for either proving or disproving a criminal case;[48] as the title of one of Leirner's sculpture series, it emphasizes the transgressive nature of the artist's activity—the unorthodoxy of her physically "appropriating" or stealing the materials for her artworks. Leirner, a constant international traveler whose home is São Paulo, has found it convenient to make a type of "Traveller's Folding Item,"[49] sculptures that in their lightness, simplicity, and flexibility permit easy transport. All of her works, assembled as they are from "homeless," impersonal, and now outlaw stuffs, provocatively upset conventional notions about the stable nature of property and identity as well as place.

Composed of the souvenirs or traces of Leirner's ceaseless movements, the *Corpus Delicti* series can be thought of as a self-portrait of the artist as itinerant worker. Another untitled piece, constructed from wire and luggage tags, quite clearly identifies Leirner as traveler (pl. 27). It is one of only a few works in which her name is visible (printed on the baggage tags) and for which the artist has thus provided a kind of qualified signature. That she should use an ephemeral luggage tag to "sign" her sculpture gives us a sense of the degree to which Leirner regards herself—her very identity—as an ever-shifting function of the long-distance journeys that her home in Brazil, on the periphery of the art world, has required of her. It is worth pointing out that Leirner's sculptural records of an endless journeying, migration, or circulation—and of their sudden suspension—falls squarely within a tradition of Latin American thought and art-making that is haunted by the irresolvable duality of home versus homelessness, of place versus displacement, and the encounters and conflicts that inevitably ensue.

Fig. 16.
Jac Leirner
Blue Phase, 1991
Bank notes, polyurethane cord,
and Plexiglas
Two parts, each 3 x 122 x 6 inches
(8 x 310 x 15 cm)
Collection of Jorge and Marion Helft,
Buenos Aires

To be rooted is perhaps the most important and least recognized need of the human soul.
                                                                    —Simone Weil[50]

Argentina is like a Diaspora; you are talking about no cultural background—you belong nowhere, and as a Jewish Argentine even more.
                                                                    —Guillermo Kuitca[51]

But if I have no roots, why have my roots hurt me so?
                                                                    —Alicia Duvojne Ortiz[52]

Guillermo Kuitca's paintings of maps, apartment-house plans, genealogical charts, and schemas of institutional structures are freighted with the poignant desire to ground oneself securely through the rendering of iconographic images that are evocative of location, home, or belonging. Beginning with the bed as "a place of origin, of beginning and end, and always the point of departure"[53] (first as an image in his paintings, subsequently as the literal support for a number of his works), Kuitca's pieces exhibit the frail traces of unattained and perhaps unattainable places or relationships. His diagrammatic images are always one step removed from reality and actual experience; they therefore necessarily intimate a sense of distance at the same time that they convey a powerful yearning for what lies beyond or elsewhere. Haunted, then, by a sense of removal or estrangement—from the intimate space of the bed, or from the circle of the family as suggested by an apartment plan, or from the communal arena mapped in city plans and geographical renderings—Kuitca's works are projections of worlds, some of them actual but most of them purely imaginary, into which we can never enter or to which we can never belong. Kuitca's images—in that they mostly resemble maps, which are intended, through their precise ordering or calibration of space, to assist in the finding of one's way, the tracing of one's lineage, or the locating of one's home—are all responses (however improbable) to an apprehension of rootlessness.

The nondescript, four-room apartment "plan" in *Planta con fondo blanco [Plan with White Background]* (pl. 25) is one from which human beings are absent, though traces of human activity underscore the desolation of the depicted scene. The home—the "frame" or container within which our formative experiences take place—is shown here as a series of rooms each locked in solitude: "the beds, the rooms, the models of apartments...are bound spaces, places of confinement and isolation...in which life is reduced to quantifiable units and bound by four walls."[54] Rather than offering any amenity or comfort, the home-place of *Planta con fondo blanco* is a stage for alienation and for the breakdown of social cohesion indispensable to domestic life. The reduction of the private domain to a few isolated rooms sealed off both from one another and from the outside, together with an almost paralyzing sense of oppression and cold-hearted surveillance conveyed by the work's "aerial" or overhead point of view, resonates profoundly within the literal context of Kuitca's own Argentinian homeland, and with Argentina's recent traumatic history: the apartment plan may be seen "ultimately [as] a symbol of the military dictatorships that have ruled Argentina intermittently since 1966, most recently from 1976 to 1983."[55] Kuitca's apartment-house plans are the visual analogues of a diminished way of life, constrained by the omnipotent eye of an absolute authority. Still, though, fragile traces of human life are here and there caught within the apartment-house outlines or boundaries, traces indicative of an activity redemptively outside the inert, proscribed, mundane, and anonymous structures actually pictured.

Untitled (People on Fire) and *The Tablada Suite I* (pl. 24) are likewise trenchant social images. Diagrammatically mapping relationships between otherwise isolated individuals which together cumulatively constitute a kind of collective portrait, both paintings delineate sets of "psychic landmarks"[56] as opposed to specific geographic locales. Implicit in the family chart and in the schema of the civic structure—in the very spectral delicacy of their rendering as well as in their given imagery—is a "dread of loneliness"[57]: the fear of a deracination literally experienced by Kuitca's Russian-Jewish grandparents when they fled to Argentina, and inherited as a spiritual legacy by the artist. Kuitca's work is deeply engaged with the peculiar knowledge or understanding of "those persons not having a background...[or] a name without a background."[58] Added to the artist's personal awareness of multiple heritages and therefore geographies—to his sense of simultaneously belonging and not belonging to any one place—is his sharp awareness of how in Argentina, as elsewhere in Latin America, "histories of dispossession, fragmentation, and displacement [have] become the unstable ground for the formation of identity."[59] That Argentina, like all other countries for that matter, has been and continues to be built on the never-ending migration, irruption, and disappearance of various peoples makes a consciousness of displacement and the desire for place all the more acute. A radical response to such consciousness of displacement is *The Tablada Suite I*, which outlines a labyrinthian "city"[60]: a Jewish cemetery located in the suburbs of Buenos Aires, Kuitca's home city. Individually specified by sequentially numbered, boxlike rooms are the "citizens of a No-Place," who, like us, given the condition of our twentieth-century world, "[carry] out a solitary and mutually incomprehensible life on some or another ghostly periphery."[61] Loss, if not utter obliteration, is the message of this collective resting-place. Yet Kuitca's city of the dead is also an irrevocable abode and place, however qualified, of redemption, a "nowhere" which at the same time is an obdurately final "home." Such "heterotopias"[62] are a favorite setting for the writings of the Argentinian Jorge Luis Borges, a major influence upon Kuitca's own work; and both writer and artist are devoted to a cognitive mapping—however frail, vulnerably distended or fraught, or fictitious—that attempts, almost to the point of absurdity, to classify, clarify, and thereby ground "the wild profusion of existing things."[63] It matters neither to Borges nor to Kuitca that their poetically salvaging acts of classification are perforce restricted by the inherent limits of their chosen forms of taxonomy or representation.

Perhaps there's no return for anyone to a native land— only field notes for its reinvention.

—James Clifford[64]

Generally a two-dimensional field of signs symbolically transcribing three-dimensional reality, a map is an expedient (and necessarily inaccurate) tool for apprehending the world, and for charting and/or locating unfamiliar places. Maps, however, have long been understood to be in no way purely objective instruments; rather, they reveal perhaps more about the map-maker and his or her methods of structuring than they do about the external universe. We find in them not an objective reality but a mirror—a projection—both of our own biases and habits of mental organization and of our epic's particular sociocultural, political, and historical formulations.[65] Latin American artists seem uniquely sensitive to the charged nature of maps: hence we find, in 1936, the Uruguayan artist Joaquín Torres-García inverting a map of South America (fig. 17) to emphasize figuratively the power and independence of the "School of the South" and "announc[e] the end of the colonial period of Latin American art and the beginning of a new artistic era."[66] If we recognize that Latin America, before ever being sighted by the European explorers, was conceived through fanciful cartographies designed to establish the land-claims of powerful sovereigns and would-be colonizers, then we can begin to understand Kuitca's map paintings as in part a clever inversion of the history of conquest in Latin America.[67] From Kuitca's position in Buenos Aires, it is now the native South American inhabitant who may survey

Europe and record the faraway "exotic" lands he has "rediscovered" imaginatively as well as experientially. As do ancient maps, *San Juan de la Cruz* (pl. 23) mingles "home" and "abroad," the known and the unknown, the predilections of the map-maker and the envisioned foreign geography: the name of the city San Juan de la Cruz appears over and over again within the map of a region of Poland. "Traveling" (if only in mind) like the artists/surveyors who once marched alongside the explorers,[68] Kuitca causes, by means of his private associations and fantasies, otherwise heterodox and irreconcilable domains to merge, to coexist provocatively.

It is significant that Kuitca painted *San Juan de la Cruz* on upholstered mattress material, using the mattress buttons or studs to emphasize the city's repetitive appearance.[69] This material returns us to one of Kuitca's earliest leitmotifs, the bed, "a person's most personal, familiar geographical space, the first and last we have."[70] Thus Kuitca folds into the same image two contradictory spaces: one that is intimate, close, and static; and one that is enormous, distant, and fluid. Where the bed offers a primal image of dwelling or stopping, the map stands as a symbol of endless travel; fused together, map and bed describe "a world where the two experiences are less and less distinct."[71] The most intimate and most remote geographies come together in *San Juan de la Cruz* in the circulatory patterns of roads and highways, which assume the appearances of arteries and veins threading through a human body. Actual landmarks are subsumed by what can only be acknowledged as an individual's bed-time dreamscape. In this and other Kuitca works, identity and geographic place, whether literal or metaphorical, are finally inseparable—if continually displaced—entities. Kuitca makes it terribly clear that self-knowledge becomes an exacting imaginative exercise in mapping the varied conceptual landscapes one never ceases to inhabit.

Fig. 17.
Joaquín Torres-García (Uruguayan, born 1874)
Inverted Map of South America, 1936
Ink drawing reproduced in *Circulo y cuadrado I,* May 1936
Courtesy Cecilia de Torres, Ltd., New York

He turned to the flyleaf of the geography and read what he had written there: himself, his name and where he was.

Stephen Dedalus
Class of Elements
Clongowes Wood College
Sallins
County Kildare
Ireland
Europe
The World
The Universe

—James Joyce[72]

Whether offering up an image of the microscopic world caught in the mapping of a spider's web (see pl. 3) or an image of the farther bounds of the cosmos (see pl. 1), each of **Vija Celmins**'s paintings carries us in one swift and succinct stroke from the intimate fact of painted surface to the outermost reaches of mental comprehension. Unlike Joyce's young narrator, however, Celmins effortlessly voids all the steps in between, and ultimately even cancels the final location—the starry night sky, the spider's forsaken "universe," or the desert's vastness (see pl. 2)—by making these things or places inseparable from their canvas's surface or human manufacture. As if Celmins's works equipped us with a rare optical instrument, we are able to see at once magnificently *and* meticulously, but we are also always brought forcibly back to the means by which these things and places are represented, and therefore to their artificiality, if not their untruth.

Fig. 18.
Jasper Johns (American, born 1930)
Shade, 1959
Encaustic on canvas with objects
52 x 39 inches (132.1 x 99.1 cm)
Collection Ludwig, Aachen

The subjects of all Celmins's paintings are derived from photographs, and the flawless vacancy of the night-sky works is due in part to her use of satellite photos for their models. Thus, her paintings, though replete with a certain kind of apparently "naturalistic" detail, bear no direct relation to nature whatsoever. The fact that they are frequently monochrome and, despite the voluminous reach of their imagery, fixed in an adamant flatness, further signals their source in black-and-white photography. In her consistent choice of two-dimensional, necessarily already mediated images for transcription onto given two-dimensional surfaces, Celmins looks, unconsciously or not, to the grave but whimsical literalism invented by Jasper Johns (see fig. 18): since paintings are literally flat surfaces they can only logically incorporate a literally and intrinsically flat imagery (such as maps, blueprints, symbols, and signs).[73] And, not unlike the early domination of monochrome—of black and white and gray—in Johns's paintings (a banishment of color indicative of the shutting-down of representational potential), the monochrome nature of so many of Celmins's works is uniquely suited to communicate a majestic, *and* qualified, sterility. They are both beautiful inoperative outer spaces traversed only by mind and equally inoperative, absolute and mediated flatlands constructed by the artist's hand.

Perhaps, though, what is most striking about Celmins's works—and what brings us at least half-reassuringly back to "place" or home—is the technique of their manufacture. Through a painstaking process of laying down a dense field of minute marks, the artist rebuilds, as if in stubborn defiance of the very "nothingness" she paints, the new universe projected in each of her paintings. This method of construction or generation seems imitative of nature: as though Celmins would have her work be every bit as

marvelously exacting, comprehensive, and thus finally durable as the processes blindly employed by nature for the making of its geological, astrophysical, or inorganic products. Grain by grain, drop by drop, filament by filament, through an obsessive mark-making that becomes for the viewer as well absorbingly hypnotic, Celmins engenders an alternative cosmos that both serves to locate or "place" us, however shakily or provisionally, and provides us with a visually concrete equivalent for an internal state: for the most detached and wide-roaming meditation. In this process, Celmins herself seems involved: her excrutiating focus—every micromillimeter of canvas, however illusionistically distant, is held up in an aching clarity—transforms her paintings, as Celmins herself has said, into "records of mindfulness."[74] "Mindfulness," however, not only as an utter fixity of attention, but also as a will to deep and broad understanding.

The exactitude or exquisiteness of Celmins's renderings has the peculiar effect of slowing first the artist's and our attention and then seemingly her imagery's very rate of existence. Our experience of her paintings—fundamentally uniform all-over fields—is radically decelerated, causing us to become hyperaware of both *what we see* and *where* we stand in relation to it.[75] The geography charted in any one of Celmins's works, however pictorially remote and inert, suddenly snaps into immediate proximity and pressuring presence. Her uptilted surfaces, all without horizon lines, may cast us adrift in spatially ambiguous landscapes empty of navigational markers—the stars or web's threads no help at all, serving only to disorient and confuse—but these surfaces also, so laden with touch, stolidly confront and even to some extent obstruct us. That the places

Celmins chooses to project are seemingly timeless or eternally ongoing, scoured pictorially free of any dramatic and/or human incident by which they might be dated, and recorded with an almost scientific objectivity, paradoxically reinforces their impression of *absolute* presentness. We are thus contradictorily given in all her paintings absolute presence (Celmins's marks) in tandem with absolute absence (her imagery's utter illusoriness); material flatness with unfathomable representational depth; comfortingly specific detail with unsettling generalization; concreteness with incorporeality; abstraction with representation. That Celmins has been able to fuse these polar opposites and to do so within the confines of relatively small-scale paintings is the source of her art's finely strung tension.

Touch or marking, then, replaces all the supposed landmarks of the natural world as the object and/or instrument by which we can humanly negotiate space and which both literally and figuratively secures us. Celmins's "sublime" is not an external given or even an external imagined, but a laboriously fabricated and always self-qualifying construct. Her vast spaces, micro- or macrocosmic, are thus nothing more or less than mirrors or images of the mind itself, at once sweepingly capacious and lovingly attached to detail, as revealed through the hand's activity. The clarity and specificity of Celmins's mark-making has a not unlikely counterpart in Vermeer's stilled and luminous domestic interiors (see fig. 19), for, just as the globes and maps and letters from abroad introduce into his rooms imaginary vastnesses, so do the depicted stars and webs and desert surfaces of Celmins's facture. Celmins herself has quoted Czeslaw Milosz: "Imagination can [and does] fashion a homeland."[76]

Fig. 19.
Jan Vermeer (Dutch, 1632–1675)
Woman in Blue Reading a Letter,
c. 1662–64
Oil on canvas
18¼ x 15⅜ inches (46.5 x 39 cm)
Rijksmuseum, Amsterdam

Fig. 20.
June 29, 1994—A sailboat with 155 Haitian refugees aboard sits idle in the water as they await a U.S. Coast Guard cutter, the USCG *Hamilton*, to pick them up.

You have had, and have, plenty of public events and facts and general statistics of America;—in the following... is a common individual New World private life... amid the United States of America...and the lights and shades and sights and joys and pains and sympathies common to humanity.

—*Walt Whitman*[77]

Untitled (America) by **Felix Gonzalez-Torres**, the artist's largest light-string installation to date, bears a parenthetical title that provides the viewer with an interpretive point of entry. Gonzalez-Torres is unabashedly enamored of "America" (a denomination in which he includes his native Cuba, the United States, where he now lives, and Canada, the home of his longtime partner), a geographical concept as well as a place with and in which the artist has been very happy. For Gonzalez-Torres, the image of America is redolent with associations of love, celebration, and travel. In fact, the idea of travel, upon which much of Gonzalez-Torres's work revolves, alone invokes sensations of longing, hope, transience, loss, and recovery, which in turn tend to color each piece. Such associations and feelings are personal and have been encouraged by the artist's particular history; yet they are also fundamentally universal in nature and have been made all the more accessible to any viewer through Gonzalez-Torres's dextrous use of imagery. Travel for Gonzalez-Torres first took the form of immigration: born in Cuba and raised

in San Juan, Puerto Rico, Gonzalez-Torres arrived in the United States in the late 1970s at age eleven to settle in New York (where he became an artist, a teacher, and a founding member of Group Material, an art collective whose works focus on social issues). Gonzalez-Torres's background has undoubtedly influenced his sensitivity to the migrant condition.

And just beyond the frontier between "us" and the "outsiders" is the perilous territory of not-belonging: this is to where in a primitive time peoples were banished, and where in the modern era immense aggregates of humanity loiter as refugees and displaced persons.

—*Edward Said*[78]

Gonzalez-Torres knows that travel can take other forms less palatable than lawful passage, such as exile (whether voluntary or involuntary) or illegal immigration. Addressing these other forms of "travel," he has produced works that metaphorically acknowledge or otherwise lend dignity to this often painful, nomadic condition. *Untitled (Passport II)* (fig.21) is a Minimalist stack of "documents," each a little book fabricated by the artist; but instead of containing the official records that the work's subtitle suggests, these books are winsomely imprinted with images of clouds and soaring birds. Free for the viewer's taking, Gonzalez-Torres's "passports" provide the *real* missing paperwork (as opposed to the artificial official version) in which the holder is promised travel unfettered and entries unbounded by restrictive definitions of nationality or ethnicity. Such official definitions have on occasion turned the innocent traveler or migrant into a criminal: into an undocumented refugee or "illegal alien." Gonzalez-Torres, an avid reader of Walt Whitman, wishes himself to be a "poet of a 'democracy' not limited to Americans"; and his works, like Whitman's, are likewise dedicated to an "incarnation of what might yet be everybody's 'New World.'"[79]

In classic immigrant fashion, Gonzalez-Torres has embraced an idealistically optimistic view of America as *the* destination for people in search of a better life. Yet he also distinguishes between America as it should be and America as it is. To give artistic embodiment to the *imaginary place* of the "American Dream," Gonzalez-Torres has constructed his sculpture of white light bulbs arranged into groups of 42 on twelve 42-foot lengths of white extension cord. Used by Gonzalez-Torres as a festive and celebratory symbol, the electric light bulb is regarded by the artist as one of the great, quintessentially American inventions (not only because it was developed in the United States by Thomas Edison, but also because it possesses the practical and democratic properties of utility, affordability, and mass availability). While championing America, however, Gonzalez-Torres preserves affectionate recollections of his place of origin: *Untitled (America)* saturates the gallery with a wash of bright light evocative at once of the Caribbean sun and of the street festivals illuminated by decorative ropes and garlands of bare light bulbs in the artist's native Cuba.

There is also something classically American in the "democratic" method of installation and potentially endless reconfiguration of *Untitled (America)*. Though unseen by the viewer, the fact that Gonzalez-Torres relinquishes all control over the installation of his piece—above all, over its ultimate pattern and design—is critical to the both literal and metaphorical openness of his work. The curator or the owner of the work, without instructions from the artist, decides how the strings of light are to be placed. Made to cascade from the ceiling in illuminating rivulets or to dangle in festoons against the walls, Gonzalez-Torres's light strings may conjure up joy; or, just as easily, abandoned to piles on the floor, they may communicate an impression of melancholy and loss (see pls. 10–11). Willingly—even happily—exposed by Gonzalez-Torres to varying contexts and (re)interpretations, *Untitled (America)* answers in part the artist's fer-

vent desire for dialogue and community—for others taking part in the metaphorical and literal evolution of his work's meaning, which thereby gains a kind of perpetually renewed relevance and life.[80]

I find that this installation is primarily concerned with vulnerability, the state of having nothing to lose, the possibility for renewing each work every time it is contemplated by the viewer. It also constitutes a comment on the passing of time and the possibility of erasure or disappearance. . . . This work also touches upon life in its most radical definition, its limit: death. As with all artistic practices, it is related to the act of leaving one place for another, one which proves perhaps better than the first.[81]

Gonzalez-Torres's invitation to others to participate actively in the creation of his work, together with his choice of the fragile, fugitive, but endlessly replenishable light bulb as his primary material, signal another aspect of the artist's art and life: his preoccupation with the devastating impact of AIDS. *Untitled (America)* does not refer solely to geography, but to the artist's memory of his companion, who lived in Toronto and died of AIDS in 1991. "In a way this 'letting go' of the work, this refusal to make a static form, a monolithic sculpture, in favor of a disappearing, changing, unstable, and fragile form was an attempt on my part to rehearse my fears of having Ross disappear day by day right in front of my eyes."[82] Our society has offered too few opportunities to memorialize and mourn the loss of those who have died of AIDS.[83] *Untitled (America)* presents us with a large, quietly defiant commemoration of vanished, vanishing, and still brightly burning life: for the light bulbs, like so many AIDS-stricken bodies, and indeed like all of us, will inevitably be extinguished. Yet the affliction and looming loss intimated by the work are also countered by its air of profound hope. In their sheer abundance and festive swoops through the gallery space, the light bulbs seem to speak vividly of renewal and regeneration. In the tradition of one strain of conceptual art (including Sol LeWitt's and Lawrence Weiner's wall drawings), there is no "original" *Untitled (America)* sculpture, only Gonzalez-Torres's initial idea, which may be passed on and variably reproduced in endless editions, through sale or gift. *Untitled (America)* is, therefore, in a sense physically unassailable; it "has no fear of being reduced, and dreads neither death nor extinction,"[84] for it is potentially capable of resurrection almost anywhere and at any time.

Fig. 21.
Felix Gonzalez-Torres
Untitled (Passport II), 1993
Offset print on paper, endless copies
Dimensions vary with installation
Collection Goetz, Munich

Historically, African-American people believed that the construction of a homeplace, however fragile and tenuous (the slave hut, the wooden shack), had a radical political dimension. Despite the brutal reality of racial apartheid, of domination, one's homeplace was the one site where one could freely confront the issue of humanization, where one could be affirmed in our minds and hearts despite poverty, hardship, and deprivation, where we could restore to ourselves the dignity denied us on the outside in the public world.... I want to speak about the importance of homeplace in the midst of oppression and domination, of homeplace as a site of resistance and liberation struggle.

—bell hooks[85]

Kerry James Marshall's new series of paintings centers its attention upon those Chicago housing projects whose names incorporate the word "garden." While these paintings, like Marshall's earlier ones, direct oblique criticism at the shortcomings of city planning, they do not wage pitched battle against urban life. Marshall respects the social idealism of which the city housing projects are one manifestation (however misguided and inadequate). Having grown up in public housing in Alabama, followed by a stay at Nickerson Gardens in Los Angeles, Marshall possesses a wealth of childhood memories that testify to the sense of community and individual responsibility to one's surroundings fostered by life in the projects: he has spoken of how, at the age of eight, he was granted access to collectively owned garden tools with which he and his older brother could tend the family's yard before moving on to care for their neighbors' in exchange for petty cash. Yet, Marshall's paintings are in no way idealized autobiographical accounts that nostalgically yearn for a return to more innocent times—although they are stimulated by a personal and cultural history of communal dedication. Nor do they disguise under a naive cloak of hope the cruel realities of contemporary urban existence—though, ironically, a number of the images in his paintings are derived from his photographs of actual "beautification projects" (see fig. 22). Rather, Marshall's compositions fuse the real and the imaginary, often with subtle political overtones, to evoke an emotionally authentic landscape.

Neither strictly realist nor idealist representations of inner-city life, Marshall's "homescapes" disabuse us of our media-based perception of the projects as dangerous, alienated, socially fragmented spaces that have been allowed to go to ruin. Instead, his works focus upon those individual and collective acts that enable the inhabitants of public housing projects to preserve their communities and, perhaps more fundamentally, their self-respect. Marshall's paintings are exemplary narratives chronicling the human capacity for self-actualization and accountability, as is apparent, for example, in *Many Mansions* (pl. 35), in which three figures are constructively bent on pruning a garden.[86] While devised by Marshall to embody a deep sense of common humanity, these paintings never lose their specific contexts; and they make compellingly concrete and plain the moral (and by extension the political) imperative behind Marshall's work. Marshall would highlight the positive power of both individual and communal "human agency"[87] and provide at once inspirational and revisionary documents of

the capacity and ability of human beings who have been culturally degraded, politically oppressed and economically exploited.... This theme neither romanticizes nor idealizes marginalized peoples. Rather it accentuates their humanity and tries to attenuate the institutional constraints on their life-chances for surviving and thriving... by digging deep in the depths of human particularities and social specificities in order to construct new kinds of connections, affinities and communities, across empire, nation, region, race, gender, age and sexual orientation.[88]

Marshall's paintings depict members of a harmoniously functioning community voluntarily engaged in various productive or restorative activities: gardening, strolling, resting, or otherwise savoring together their leisure time. By formally invoking a classical idiom long employed by artists—and above all by muralists—for the depiction of spiritual utopias as diverse as the kingdom of heaven, Elysium, Arcadia, or "the sacred grove," Marshall ennobles the humble occupations in which his inhabitants of the here truly revitalized projects are to be found. While Marshall's materials and technique may be entirely contemporary—each painting is a patchwork of topical images fashioned out of acrylic pigment and collage on unstretched canvas—stylistically and thematically these works look back to the allegorical and pastorally serene compositions of a file of painters stretching from the Sienese Duccio to Puvis de Chavannes, Gauguin, Henri Rousseau, and Diego Rivera. Continuing this line, Marshall's own paintings—most of them of a commanding size—present idealized figurative tableaux that unfold with decorous, almost hypnotic grace within a shallow, proscenium-like space.

Marshall's compositions, like, for example, that of Puvis de

Fig. 22.
Ida B. Wells Homes, Chicago

Fig. 23.
Photo study for Kerry James Marshall's
Better Homes Better Gardens

Chavannes's *Sacred Grove* (fig. 24) or Rousseau's *Snake Charmer* (fig. 25), are precisely built of distinctly contoured, basically flat forms that together describe a lucid and thus seemingly ineluctable narrative vision. The uniform handling of these forms, together with their rather static arrangement, contributes to the paintings' trance-like stillness, to the impression of poised inevitability characteristic of a classicizing, or idealizing, style. Further, by means of surrounding borders of garlands, Marshall's paintings physically distance the viewer from their stagelike scenes. The remoteness and tranquility of the setting portrayed in each work are in turn mirrored in its human figures, whose arrested poses and introspective gazes partake of "iconic inactivity."[89] There is something otherworldly in these figures' eternally unruffled response to everyday reality—they seem untouched by the forces of either gravity or degradation—which removes them finally from the quotidian and bestows on them a larger-than-life "allegorical or symbolic status."[90] Where, then, Puvis de Chavannes's Music and Poetry languidly float through a sylvan setting peopled by the muses and the personifications of the arts, or where Rousseau's birds and serpents (so devoid of naturalistic detail as to be obviously if enigmatically symbolic) gather to an orphic flute, in Marshall's *Many Mansions* "bluebirds of happi-

ness"[91] waft past solemn, almost lapidary figures whose generalized features seem capable of belonging only to an Everyman or an Everywoman.

The "garden" titles of Marshall's subjects signal the artist's indebtedness to a long literary and artistic tradition of pastoral representation for his own vision of a contemporary urban arcadia. Imaginatively documenting a symbiotic harmony between human figures and their settings or environments—a harmony utterly at odds with the viewer's expectations—Marshall applies the vocabulary of "utopian forms that constitute a better or ideal society"[92] to the often ragged and resistant circumstances of everyday life in the projects. What is radical and refreshing about his art is precisely its translation of ordinarily overlooked or even untouchable subject matter—that is, lower middle- and middle-class existence and its quietly persistent values—into the realm of the ideal and ideally perdurable. Marshall posits for us an African-American urban community no longer contaminated or constrained by the relentless oppression, exploitation, and despair that have irrevocably shaped black American experience, a community, moreover, that has harnessed its uniquely difficult legacy for uniquely positive ends.

Marshall has stated that his "work attempts to sustain a

Fig. 24.
Pierre Puvis de Chavannes
(French, 1824–1898)
The Sacred Grove Beloved of the Arts and of the Muses, 1884–89
Oil on canvas
36⁷/₁₆ x 90¹⁵/₁₆ inches (93 x 231 cm)
The Art Institute of Chicago, Potter Palmer Collection, 1922.445

Fig. 25.
Henri Rousseau (French, 1844–1910)
The Snake Charmer, 1907
Oil on canvas
66¹/₂ x 74³/₈ inches (169 x 189 cm)
Musée d'Orsay, Paris

relationship with traditional folkways."[93] And, if his paintings display a deliberate formal connection—in their decorative patterning, highly stylized figuration, and shallow pictorial space—to earlier black folk art, then, too, their poetically luminous vision of a recovered harmony betrays a deeper *African* legacy. This legacy is most evident in the nondidactic and tranquilly rapt way Marshall's compositions effortlessly blend the real and the marvelous. Tellingly, Marshall's reliance on allegory and symbolism for the development of a pictorial narrative closely links his work to that of independent black filmmakers, who also characteristically convey an almost otherworldly "unrushed wholeness that imparts stature and dignity."[94] Marshall himself has served as production designer for a number of socially conscious and entrancing films (including *Daughters of the Dust* and *Sankofa*)[95] for which he transformed the setting—usually a dwelling-place—or *mise-en-scène* itself into a crucial dramatic character. His method was to utilize objects and props that symbolically reverberated with latter-day echoes of ancient African belief systems and lore. Unquestionably, Marshall's paintings are influenced by the artist's intimate knowledge of film, an inalienably narrative art form, and of film's theatrical devices and effects. Marshall's work, "hopeful rather than accurate"[96] and at core celebratory, brings a ritualized style of representation to screen *and* canvas that has enabled his imagery to hover between the real and the imaginary. His paintings project a place at once mythic and topically concrete, a place imbued with "intellectual rigor, existential dignity, moral vision, political courage and soulful style."[97]

The work of **Jeff Wall**, which shares with Kerry James Marshall's an indebtedness to modern cinema as well as to the history of European painting, brings aspects of both art forms to bear suggestively on the artist's vision of the contemporary urban landscape. Like Marshall, Wall populates his works with life-size emblematic figures, the expression of whose identities is largely prescribed by their settings—by "place"—and who are the protagonists of narratives that are as much artful allegory as pointed reportage. Wall's pieces, which formally are hybrids of photography, cinema, and painting,[98] recall at first glance movie stills—arrested dramatic moments within ongoing stories—while the artist's working method (in its conceptualization, the research for its subject and props, "location scouting" and "character casting," shooting schedule and editing process, and a collaborative approach to the works' realization) borrows heavily from filmmaking. Furthermore, each completed Wall photograph—a very large, high-resolution cibachrome transparency back-lit by fluorescent lights and set into a display case—is intended to capture and involve the viewer's attention in much the way the images projected onto movie screens do. Importantly, this large-scale, self-illuminated format, which Wall has used consistently since 1978, is common to commercial display as well as to film. Yet, while Wall may employ devices of visual persuasion familiar to us from advertising and movies, he does so not to conjure tantalizing and perfected dream images of escapist desire, but, conversely, to lay bare critically and vividly the all-too-real raw underside of our late industrial society.

Wall's works adopt strictly contemporary modes of visual address—the look and technology of the movie frame or still, of the photo-advertisement, of the documentary photograph—in order to recontextualize and thus reinvigorate the classic Western pictorial idiom. This idiom, exemplified preeminently by the dramatic figure painting of the last five centuries, is shown in Wall's pieces to be a language still capable of relevance, still capable of delivering substantive meaning with incomparable bite. Carefully deploying form, shape, color, line, and light in accordance with established compositional principles, Wall engages in a grave, unironical dialogue with art history and sees his photo-installations as the direct offspring of earlier Western painting.[99] Wall's belief in the continuing viability of painting separates him from most photo-conceptual artists of the 1970s to 1990s, many of whom have mounted in their works a blistering critique of the pictorial tradition and its formal strictures, calling for their dismantling or deconstruction. For Wall, on the other hand, Western painting is a deeply engrafted humanist project, both inevitable and necessary, a project that no mere "critique of representation" can lightly dislodge.

He is looking for that quality which you must allow me to call "modernity".... He makes it his business to extract from fashion whatever element it may contain of poetry within history, to distill the eternal from the transitory.... Often weird, violent and excessive, he has contrived to concentrate... the acrid or heady bouquet of the wine of life.

—*Charles Baudelaire*[100]

Thematically, Wall subscribes to the central tenet of modernity identified by Charles Baudelaire in the mid-nineteenth century and embodied in the paintings of Baudelaire's contemporaries, artists such as Edouard Manet, Gustave Caillebotte, and Edgar Degas. In the manner of these nineteenth-century urban Impressionists, as refracted, however, through the prism of a socialist brand of art history,[101] Wall applies a knowledge of the Western pictorial tradition to the critical reexamination of contemporary life. His works observe human subjects (or their allegorical substitutes) caught in the common places of day-to-day urban existence and chronicle "the conflicts involved in making the [modern] city,"[102] conflicts that irrevocably transform not only the city's physical fabric, but also its mostly vulnerable inhabitants.[103] Like his Impressionist predecessors, Wall focuses upon archetypically "modern" cityscapes—for Caillebotte and Manet this cityscape was Haussmann's mid-nineteenth-century Paris; for Wall it is the fringe environments of "second" cities like Tijuana, Mexico, and Vancouver (the artist's home) where the forces of late capitalism are most crudely dramatized.[104] Wall's chosen locations have been wholly shaped by the exigencies of modernism: by the enforced migration of large groups of people, the collision of different cultures within soulless and/or derelict no-man's-land spaces, and of individual identity deracinated to the point that community is only a chimera and the ordinary mode of social "encounter" one of territorial defensiveness.

An Encounter in the Calle Valentín Gómez Farías, Tijuana (pls. 52–53) might at first glance seem the straightforward documentation of an everyday scene. The encounter takes place in the late morning hours of an unexceptionally sunny day in Tijuana, where a narrow rubble street is seen to descend sharply from an invisible highway above. The street, which cascades into a hidden canyon converted by dint of human labor and social necessity into a poor *colonia*, or neighborhood, terminates at a point where a dog and a chicken stand at a suspicious distance from each other. Though the *colonia* is in reality inhabited by freely roaming dogs and chickens, this particular encounter was carefully choreographed by Wall using trained animals. Despite the casual "slice of life" look of *An Encounter*, the photograph's contents have been compositionally organized to recast a telling moment of raw, commonplace life in the heightened language of the Western pictorial tradition. Wall's image displays, as might a Baroque painting, a high horizon line from which descend dynamic, zig-zagging axialities connotative both of turbulent movement and of emotional upset. Here, the agitated and disorderly setting, much like the background of a traditional allegorical painting, serves to underline the central drama depicted in its foreground. Wall has chosen one object—the corner of a wood scaffold atop a vehicle at the photograph's left—by which to guide the viewer's eye into the space of the picture. The scaffold's grid *looks* like, as well as functions as, an optical aid to perspectival rendering. Its recessive lines are picked up by the thin dirt path that moves upwards and diagonally across the picture plane, circumnavigating a dark mound which in turn acts as a weighty frame or ceiling pressing the eye back down to the foreground clearing where the dog and hen meet.

By such relatively sophisticated compositional devices, we are made to recognize the hen and the dog as allegorical figures vividly embodying an archetypal episode of *human* social relations frequently met with in cities or in places of transit and passage. A similar, if far more subdued encounter (or rather lack thereof) is the subject, for instance, of Gustave Caillebotte's magnificent pictorial machine *Paris Street; Rainy Day* (fig. 26), which depicts a Parisian crossroads captured at a moment of casual discord or estrangement between not two different animals, but three emphatically distinct human beings about to cross paths. "Encountering" someone other, whether disconcertingly unlike *or* like oneself, is to experience a temporary destabilization or voiding of identity. The protagonists of Wall's and Caillebotte's works, be they dog and hen or two men and a woman, are made acutely aware of their respective isolation, dispossession, and strangeness within the *terrain-vague* of the city. In *An Encounter* as in *Paris Street; Rainy Day*, the main figures are pictorially crowded toward the foreground within a "walled" space that belies and throws into sharp relief the unbridgeable—or barely bridgeable—distance that prevails between them, a distance endemic to modern city life.[105] Wall, like Caillebotte before him, suspends the moment of this encounter (or, in Caillebotte's case, avoidance of an encounter) to arrive at a hypnotically tense and troubling image of unresolved alienation. Such dramatic moments are the charged beginnings of territorial marking, including the territory of an inviolate personal space, and of the endless negotiation of movement that the city demands.

Equally a subject of *An Encounter* is the place of the street itself, a *calle* selected by Wall after a period of thorough location scouting. Of all the places Wall might choose for the making of his photographs, he has steadfastly trained his camera upon unremarkable residual spaces—"the interstices...the 'dead zones,' the streets and empty backlots...the conduits of the everyday"[106]—where things, unordered and unpoliced, simply flow and where unlikely encounters and potential conflicts are bound to occur. In its searing details, however, the street *in An Encounter* bears the presence of a particular personality. It is built up of rubble and flanked by temporary housing; it is eroded yet oddly dignified by the name of the Mexican war hero Valentín Gómez Farías. As such, Calle Valentín Gómez Farías is a microcosm of the conditions peculiar to so-called "developing" nations—to northern Mexico and to Tijuana in particular—conditions that, while largely international in origin, have resulted in "one of the great[est] human migrations in history."[107] The *calle*, like Tijuana itself and like Paris a century earlier, is a place undergoing cataclysmic change—a place in and of transition—riven by social collapse and by extensive architectural either "renewal" or ruin. Yet the *calle*, along which a lonely figure labors toward the road's apex, is also revitalized by a sense of unfaltering human determination. This figure, like perhaps the man walking head bent across Caillebotte's grand *place*, is about "resistance, survival, communication and...dialogue."[108]

Fight on the Sidewalk (pl. 51), a picture Wall composed using a Vancouver location, derives its power in large part from the formal composition of its street setting, an anonymous urban "dead space" that throws its human subjects into high relief. Here, as in *An Encounter*, the setting—a sidewalk in a canyon of buildings—both encloses and intensifies the central scene as if it were more a bleak indoor than an open outdoor drama. Within this cold, severe, and assertively modern landscape, underclass characters act out a social disintegration—the pernicious unraveling of a community fabric—dictated by advanced urbanism. *Fight on the Sidewalk*, like so many of Manet's paintings (see specifically *Philosopher [with Hat]*, fig. 27),[109] depicts an aspect of modernity that, though it wholly surrounds us, we would choose to ignore: the solitary, alienated, and poverty-stricken individuals who have suffered ruthless displacement in the wake of the city's modernization. Transformed, however, by means of their strategically composed settings into emblems of a seemingly insoluble societal inequity, these figures enable Wall to show "what's happening to people as they go through a city experience, possibly rejecting it, and how people are transformed, how some are ruined and some not ruined....to show some results of those kinds of mutations such as the immigrant experience....some of the dirt of that experience and also some of the potential of it."[110]

In allowing the central figures of each of his photographic compositions to be almost life size, and in positioning them close to the picture's surface, Wall contrives for us *a physical* relation to his image and thereby psychologically projects us into its space. The dissociation and embattled isolation he has caused both his characters and their settings to embody allegorically becomes the salient experience for the viewer as well. It is this visceral connection between viewer and image that is the final and necessary element of completing any one of Wall's works, for "the key experience for modernist art is this dissociation of identity, I think. In it, we see both our actual existence for what it is and, at the same time, catch a glimpse of something extremely different. Something better."[111] With it, Wall succeeds in what Baudelaire deemed the paramount achievement of the "Painter of Modern Life": the ability to compellingly "interpret the age to itself."[112]

Fig. 26.
Gustave Caillebotte (French, 1848–1894)
Paris Street; Rainy Day, 1877
Oil on canvas
83½ x 108¾ inches
(212.2 x 276.2 cm)
The Art Institute of Chicago, Charles H. and Mary F. S. Worcester Collection, 1964.336

Fig. 27.
Edouard Manet (French, 1832–1883)
The Philosopher (with Hat), 1865–67
Oil on canvas
74 x 43³⁄₁₆ inches (188 x 109.8 cm)
The Art Institute of Chicago, Arthur Jerome Eddy Memorial Collection, 1931.504

It's remarkable how often one hears it stubbornly repeated that formalism is congenitally antipathetic to history. I myself have always tried to state the historical responsibility of forms.
—*Roland Barthes*[113]

I think of Marden's paintings as rigorous attempts to bring into physical and visual proximity the essences (the cross fertilizations) of a day's light, a place's history, a place's sky and earth and walls, paintings as both a physical plane and insubstantial image, and the yearning that informs all great painting.
—*John Yau*[114]

Brice Marden's perceptual art is grounded in a highly private and often seemingly tactile experience of both physical and imaginary worlds. Marden's works do not so much describe as evoke human and geographic forms—"people" and "places" charged with personal meaning for their maker. Marden's chosen subjects or "surroundings," whether literal, metaphorical, art historical, or otherwise, are repeatedly subjected to a process of re-imagining by which they are transformed into abstract paintings, each the physical equivalent of "a highly subjective state."[115] Describing within their borders "a site or a location at once generously allusive *and* self-referential,"[116] Marden's canvases have always loosely taken their cue from the imaginatively distilled essences of their artist's particular environment. His earliest paintings—introspective, mute, and apparently imperturbable—derived not only their scale but also their emotional shading from the human body; the layers of at once subtly mottled and thickly impervious encaustic paint coating the surfaces of these works have been described by Marden as "a dumb skin over an essence."[117] The later, "post-and-lintel" paintings (1979–85) similarly, if also differently, point explicitly back to the archetypal elements of architectural (i.e., man-made) structures. In the artist's most recent body of paintings, the viewer's eye and imagination are set adrift among multifarious imagistic associations that waver between the molecular, the organic, the architectural, and the figural, but which perhaps most constantly suggest the generative formal structures underlying all earthly matter. The titles of the paintings exhibited in "About Place" are indicative of some of Marden's points of departure: for example, the human body generally speaking (*Corpus*, pl. 34), or the artist's two daughters (*The Sisters*, pl. 32). Larger works of the last few years recall the landscape surrounding Marden's home (specifically, the artist's summer residence in Greece, in the painting *February in Hydra*, pl. 33); here the outdoor locale, the space of the studio and of painterly activity, and the mental map cast over both are fused into one complex (re)invocation. Intimations of landscape have, in fact, been present in nearly all Marden's work, largely due to the artist's use of distinctively muted earth, water, and foliage colors.

The singular effect achieved through the painting technique Marden has evolved over the last ten years ties his recent work yet more closely to the concept of place. Marden's method involves a flattening—that is also a dematerializing—of every paint stroke applied to his canvas grounds through the alternating acts of drawing with paint and of sanding, scraping, and wiping down his already thinly washed surfaces; the result is "a shalelike consolida-

tion of strata laminated to the flatness of the plane."[118] Critical to this process is the visible preservation of every mark the artist has executed, even when certain marks or lines are subsequently annulled or "whited out." Marden "cancels"[119] such seemingly unwelcome lines by overpainting with a whitish pigment that has been mixed with the lines' original colors; paradoxically his "erasures" (which are not really erasures at all), corrections, and modifications function as integral and positive compositional elements—"active, composed—that is, painted, drawn"[120]—however negative the cancellations may at first appear, however ghostly and elusive the resulting image may seem.[121] These carefully drafted cancellations or adjustments help modulate each work's painted network of lines and its surface ground so that both are rendered as one fully and subtly intertwined fabric or tissue. The entire canvas becomes an undulating field of innumerable chromatically as well as gesturally related linear weavings and interweavings, a bed of emerging and dissolving continuous marks and congruent colors knitting the work into a compositional whole of striking presence.

As a consequence of his technique, the making of Marden's paintings cannot be chronologically unraveled: so consolidated and texturelessly smooth are their surfaces, so interlaced are their matrices of illusionary lines, that his works subvert any traditional notion of order or sequence, either between paler (and thus "'chromatically' further away in space [and time]")[122] and darker, or between "figure" (or form) and "ground." Instead, past and present, far and near, are made perceptually ambiguous in such a way that "the temporal and spatial orders"[123] are entirely suspended. More specifically, the collapse of time—the time not only of "process" or of the paintings' generation, but also suggestively the time reaching back to the archaeological—within the borders of any one painting conveys an impression of at once eternal presentness *and* eternal remove. "Place" in a Marden painting is in turn fixed at the juncture of encounter between viewer and artwork—between inside and outside, here and there, now and then, self and other—at which moment, however fleeting, both viewer and work are uniquely defined or located.

Marden's line seems utterly of the moment, in part because of its apparent tenuousness, hesitancy, continual dissolution, and rematerialization. It is, in fact, a vehicle not only of statement but of self-qualification and the explicitly hindered gesture. The critic and poet John Yau has provided a succinct description:

From the outset of his career, Marden accepted the inevitability of being continuously thwarted, of never being able to arrive at a purely spiritual realisation. His response was to make fully considered proposals, which remain open and incomplete. It is this incompleteness, the ache of it, that haunts the paintings, the artist, and the viewer.[124]

Marden for his recent paintings has looked to the work of Jackson Pollock (see fig. 28);[125] Marden, however, has necessarily approached the expansive fields of Pollock's paintings through the introspective and chastened viewpoint first articulated in the works of Jasper Johns.[126] Ever since Johns's earliest maps and targets, both abstract and figurative painting have been fertilely wracked by an

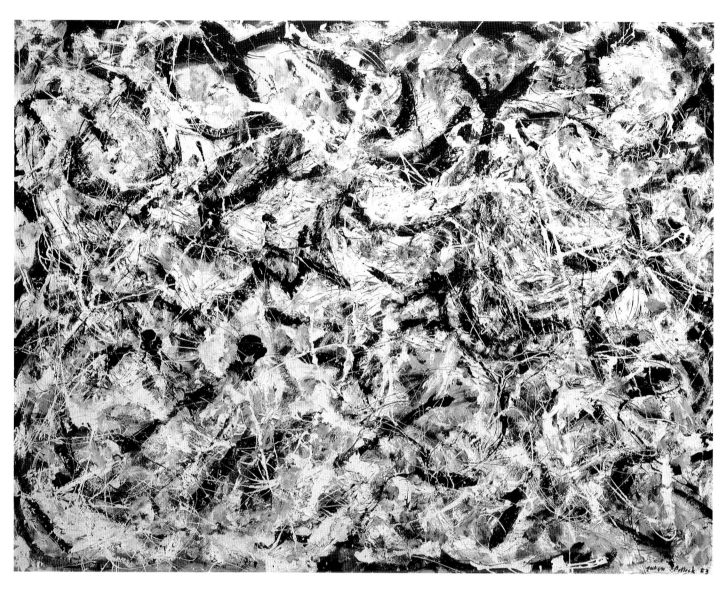

Fig. 28.
Jackson Pollock
(American, 1912–1956)
Grayed Rainbow, 1953
Oil on canvas
72 x 96 inches (182.9 x 243.8 cm)
The Art Institute of Chicago, Gift of the
Society for Contemporary Art,
1955.494

inner antagonism in which a critical self-reflexivity acknowledges the impossibility of ever getting beyond the material facts of pigment and canvas and thus beyond the *illusoriness* of all imaging: that is, the impossibility of ever arriving at a "pure" or "direct" manifestation of a figure, a thought, a spiritual urge or apprehension on the painting's two-dimensional plane. Without denying either the uses of or the deeply ingrained need for *representation*, Johns's work nevertheless radically altered the context within which painting—Marden's included—can now be conducted. Thus, while Marden's works may, like Pollock's, create an all-over pattern indicative of " a continuous surrounding space of no known depths or limits, a space that is thus, for all the supposed formal purity of content, quintessentially metaphysical,"[127] they are also deliberately marred—literally as well as metaphorically revised, rerouted, scratched out, abraded—by an awareness that these paintings cannot in any actual sense embody sublimity and grandeur. In lieu of Pollock's "strenuously sustained self-assurance,"[128] Marden's art offers an apparently (though *only* apparently) more modest ambition—the desire to incorporate a sustained consciousness of art-making's very limitations, which is an inescapable aspect of our "place" and age.

> The very idea of a definitive gesture, or even a typical one, is contrary to the ambitions of our time.... There are no movements to be championed, or paradigms to be elected; there is no air of inevitability around which a history might be composed. Nor are such lacunae incidental to the art that in fact exists. Our present esthetic modesty, and its corresponding critical restraint, are symptoms of a deeper uncertainty.
>
> —Jim Lewis[129]

The cancellations, dematerializations, discontinuities, and ruptures of which Marden's works are paradoxically constituted may be considered indicative of the uncertainty of contemporary cultural values and existence. The only sincere gesture seemingly left in a Marden painting is one that would literally negate or erase itself at the very moment of its making. Yet, despite the now settled suspicion of images and image-making, Marden's works still evidence their maker's determination to pursue certain ideas central to the tradition of abstract painting—ideas Marden still considers crucial to the conception of his art. His paintings may announce the relativity of all mark-making, of direct expression, identity, and place, but they do so without ever outright abolishing any one of them. Though fragile, vulnerable, and provisional, Marden's paintings—each a "proposal"—construct a location at once personal and metaphorical: "the work as a place of formation."[130]

For Marden, "place" has long been pinned to the human body—our most intimate "geography." Since his earliest paintings, the body has been alluded to, intimated, suggested, though never directly depicted. His most recent works invoke the body not only through their vertical, human-scale formats, but also through their stretched canvases' literal depth, which reinforces an impression of corporeality. Furthermore, Marden's paintings more or less directly bear the imprint of the artist's own body: their height and width are often such that they can be comfortably carried by Marden around his studio, and the very images they present are the hovering traces

of Marden's kinetic engagement with his materials, the traces of the reach of his body, of the specific and unique movements of his hand.[131] Finally, Marden's imagery has been repeatedly compared to the body's inner landscape: for example, to the "voyaging inside a human respiratory organ,"[132] each of his surfaces a translucent accumulation of matter and/or gesture "comparable to tissular accretions."[133] Because "the skin metaphor [has been] pervasive in Marden's early literature.... It is thus logical to look at the surface of his post-1985 canvases as that of a skinned body"[134]: in a sense, "by removing the protective skin that once encased his [pre-1985] paintings, Marden reveals the cellular organic activity governing both [his art's] life and his [own] physical being."[135] Indeed, Marden's works are grounded in a faith contracted to the unpredictable and incessantly self-modifying universe of the self; and they map, however provisionally or gropingly, a space indistinguishable at last from the ongoing articulation of individual subjectivity. It is in both the momentarily breathtaking imaginative range and the terribly severe constraints of this subjectivity, of which our Modernist predicament has made us so acutely aware, that his works find their "place," their challenge, and their solace.

> I hope when I am no longer here these pieces will stand out as statements on Black historical memory which demanded attention: not in a direct way, but in a way which allows everyone to participate and react. It is a heavy subject, and I have grown into working with material which has memory.
>
> —Leonardo Drew[136]

For his large sculptural installation, *Number 43* (pls. 8–9), **Leonardo Drew** has chosen cotton rags and other detritus such as wood, rope, canvas, and nails, all of which have been made to carry a reddish dusting of surface rust and thereby rendered chromatically harmonious and compatible. In that Drew's materials are mostly "found," and found in forsaken places like an industrial refuse dump near the housing project in Bridgeport, Connecticut, where the artist grew up, his sculptures literally arise from and resonate with a gritty but crumbling urban life and history. Furthermore, Drew's incorporation of raw and/or processed and discarded cotton in this and earlier works serves symbolically to invoke the history of the American South (Drew was born in Tallahassee, Florida) and commemorate the African and African-American plantation slaves upon whom the labor-intensive cultivation of "king cotton" once depended. As if in mimetic homage to his ancestors' labor, Drew's sculptures are all intensely worked; and they convey in their painstakingly obsessive accumulations of cast-off stuffs both the rude but fastidiously detailed handicraft and the talismanic folk mysticism of Southern black or outsider art.[137] Paradoxically, from such humble, neglected, and even disreputable materials and working methods, Drew constructs highly complex and powerfully integrated epic sculptures—wall-bound sculptures that are like panoramic barriers or dense curtain walls oriented as much toward pictorial as toward real space.

Drew's working method looks as much to postwar New York art-making as to black folk art or to an imaginary reconception of the procedural essence of Southern black labor. At a very early age, Drew became acquainted through photographs with Jackson Pollock's late "all-over" compositions. What interested him was less "the sublimated Pollock,"[138] that is, that quality of Pollock's paintings indicative either of the unconscious or an unattainable metaphysicality, than the aggressive, even violent physicality of Pollock's technique. This energy allowed not only for large "gesture," but also for the action of gravity and the irruption onto the canvas of unlikely banal materials: "a residue of 'dumping'. . . a heterogeneity of trash—nails, buttons, tacks, keys, coins, cigarettes, matches."[139] Drew learned from Pollock the potential visceral charge that the evidences of process can pack; and retaining the imprint of *his* hand or touch in a manipulation of his materials, Drew has gone on to develop a working method similarly capable of transforming gesture into art and, in this case, into *sculpture*.[140] *Number 43*, however, as an homage to consuming labor, whether voluntary or involuntary—the labor "of the slave. . . [as well as] of the artist"[141]—goes beyond being an essay in process and artistic performance to plumb persistent personal and cultural memories. Every inch of this mammoth but oddly delicate work is conspicuously touched, fingered, adjusted, manipulated, rehandled, and rethought so that *Number 43* reverberates as if it were a living body with an active residue of generative energy, vigorously entertained recollection, and ongoing desire.

Not unexpectedly, as an additional means of sharpening the vulnerable physical character of his work, Drew has made use of processes of weathering and corrosion and decay. He has, in fact, taught himself how to modulate both the rate and the intensity of rusting, employing the range of oxide or dry earth-red colors that result from his "chemistry" to arresting and often moving compositional ends. That Drew welcomes a certain controlled deterioration of his sculpture's constituent materials links his practice to that of the Italian Arte Povera school and somewhat less directly to Robert Smithson's sculptural investigations of entropy (see fig. 29). The latter's "lifelong fascination with the disorder of the industrial landscape, particularly that of his native New Jersey,"[142] also finds a parallel in Drew's interest in the outcast sites and dumping areas and the accumulating detritus of urban collapse. In *Number 43*, Drew salvaged his distressed and cast-off materials by creating for them a new domicile within the vast field of small boxlike containers comprising the sculpture. Crude stuffs, which, because they have been processed, used, worn, and roughly thrown away, inescapably evoke a sometime human presence, are gathered up by the artist and ordered, stored, arrested in their decay, and at last preserved and transformed.

Compositionally Drew's *Number 43*, not unlike a number of sculptures by Eva Hesse (see fig. 30), recasts the Minimalist grid and its structuring by systematic progression into a more vulnerable and irregular form. Drew's sculpture shares with several Hesse pieces a shallow, wall-oriented, frontal format that automatically relates these works to painting; but in Drew's case, this type

Fig. 29.
Robert Smithson
(American, 1938–1973)
Chalk-Mirror Displacement, 1987
version of a 1969 work
Sixteen mirrors and chalk
10 x 120 inches (25.4 x 304.8 cm)
diameter overall
The Art Institute of Chicago, through prior gift of Mr. and Mrs. Edward Morris, 1987.277

of arrangement—with its "frontal and diagrammatically two-dimensional look"[143]—together with the incorporation of unorthodox materials such as nails, bits of wire, string, and padded cloth, also recalls traditional African totemic forms. *Number 43* seems weighted, gravity bound, and obdurately physical, where a Hesse sculpture may seem frail as a breath. By means of its literal size and presence, *Number 43* powerfully fixes the viewer in the space he or she temporarily inhabits with the piece. In addition, the work's constituent boxlike units—each "box" visually unique from and only loosely dependent upon the next—together comprise a gridlike facade that imaginatively resembles an anonymous urban landscape or towering wall: the sculpture presents a metaphorical image of social ruin and/or frustration. Yet from the discarded "materials" of a social system founded upon a long history of racism, economic deprivation, and human waste, Drew dedicates himself to constructing, piece by piece, a redemptive and inclusive counter-order. This commanding wall is but a lively crowding of little containers, each one of them frayed, elaborately worked, and only seemingly anarchically thrown together with its companions. Every unit has been made to abut the next, precariously and provisionally, but also agreeably: gaps and fissures, crevices and perforations, announce the fact that Drew does not force a joining of divergent parts, but instead allows a chaotically variegated, yet composed, field to emerge. This method describes on its maker's part "an urge. . . to structurally, and thus fundamentally, connect or knit or

heal without, however, in the least suppressing any local particularity; to draw disparate elements together by means of a kind of thoughtfully permissive. . . association."[144] The hypnotically intricate, as well as forceful formal, arrangements that Drew constructs, and the meticulously detailed and obsessively repetitive nature of his working methods are evidence of a restless drive on this artist's part to rescue his material—which by metaphorical expansion is *all* his subject matter—and to give this material an abiding home.

Fig. 30.
Eva Hesse (American, born Germany, 1936–1970)
Sans II, 1968
Fiberglass
38 x 170¾ x 6⅛ inches
(96.5 x 433.7 x 15.6 cm)
Whitney Museum of American Art, Purchase, with funds from Ethelyn and Lester J. Honig and the Albert A. List Family

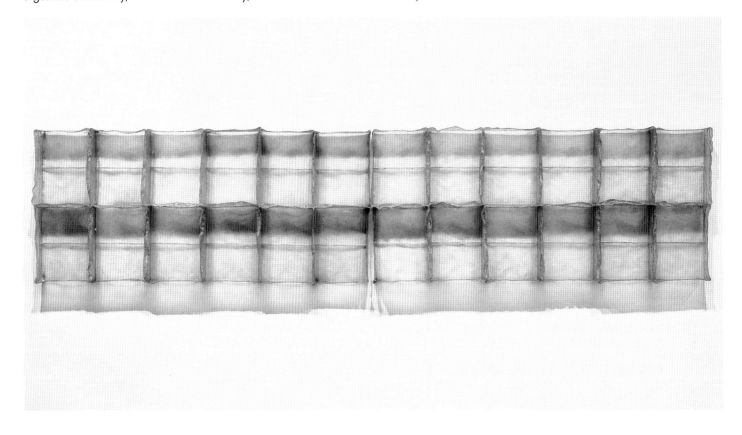

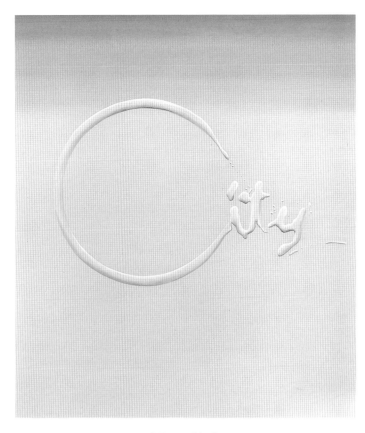

This, then, is the "full" world of America's west coast—a world of palpable light, liquid surfaces and gauzy atmospheres where nothing solid is its solid self.

—Dave Hickey[145]

Los Angeles figures prominently in **Larry Johnson**'s oeuvre as a both visual and verbal terrain. Registering the city's particular dialect—a type of speech filtered semantically and graphically through the dominant popular media—Johnson, perhaps better than any artist since Edward Ruscha in the West Coast's word-and-image tradition, literally as well as figuratively articulates the "cool" sensibility of Los Angeles via his subject matter and hard-edged style. *Standing Still & Walking in Los Angeles* (pl. 21) conveys through a specific compositional conceit the laconic urbanity of L. A. as set against a perfectly clear, inhospitably bright backdrop. *Standing Still* is a two-part composition, the left half of which spells out the work's title in a type font electronically distorted to mimic a rippling surface: the letters appear to float upon or within the liquid contents of a sun-struck pool. The right half of the work—the entire piece is a computer-generated photographic print consciously scaled to suggest a mid-sized abstract painting—exhibits the signature sign of the Abstract Expressionist idiom: the "arbitrary," gravity-bound drip, emptied of any gestural or expressive immediacy. Johnson's "messy" dispersal of subject matter across his work's surface is deliberate and representational rather than extemporaneous and direct, and he has borrowed his method of rendering from the precisionist commercial graphic techniques evolved by Hollywood's culture industry (for which Johnson himself has worked as a darkroom technician developing graphics for special effects movies). The immaculate finish of Johnson's surfaces, as well as their deliberate and ironical distancing from any expressionist emotional urgency, ties his work to that

of Ruscha, and in particular to Ruscha's so called "liquid word" paintings (1966–69), such as *City* (fig. 31).[146] Though *City* presents a painted image, while *Standing Still* is mechanically produced, both works display equally uninflected, impersonal, and meticulously crafted surfaces. Ruscha's lettering seems to enact the very liquefaction and "gravitational downfall" associated with Jackson Pollock's "drip" technique, all the while ensuring however that "pictorially speaking," the painting remains "very 'clean'…no texture, no material mark of the process."[147] Johnson similarly creates seemingly weightless and sign-filled works that are responsive to the local environment and especially to its chief industry—that is, to Los Angeles and to the celluloid and electronic media that have overwhelmed the city's modes of self-expression.[148]

Yet Johnson's work is the product of sensibility, however much it appears circumscribed by the artificial and mechanical. His photographic prints communicate a distinct "sense of indolence and ease,"[149] a mannered aestheticism that itself thrives upon and calculatedly manipulates the fine formal machinery of artifice. Much the same sensibility—the same cool distance promoted by a meticulously rendered and pristine technique, the same languid air—prevails in the work of the British expatriate, Los Angeles-based painter David Hockney (see fig. 32). Hockney's sun-shot paintings of beautiful, disengaged young men swimming in crisply delineated pools or lounging poolside on sunny stone or tile surfaces suggest the detachment, idleness, and even ennui apprehendable in Johnson's slowly undulating fonts, etiolated surfaces, and celebrity-weary voice. This avowedly artificial stance toward and view of the world has been defined by Susan Sontag as "camp."[150] But camp per se, while seemingly disengaged in attitude (and often outrageous in behavior), often in fact masks a pointed and honest criticism of society—above all, a critique of society's disregard and abusive treatment of homosexuals, for whom camp has long served as a mordant, coded language of self-legitimization and defiance.[151] Often riddled with

Fig. 31.
Edward Ruscha
(American, born 1937)
City, 1968
Oil on canvas
55 x 48 inches (139.7 x 121.9 cm)
The Art Institute of Chicago, Twentieth-Century Purchase Fund, 1969.722

Fig. 32.
David Hockney (English, born 1937)
Portrait of an Artist (Pool with Two Figures), 1972
Acrylic on canvas
84 x 120 inches (214 x 275 cm)
Collection of David Geffen,
Los Angeles

Fig. 33.
Larry Johnson
Untitled (Admit Nothing), 1994
Ektacolor photograph
45³/₄ x 58⁷/₈ inches
(116.2 x 149.5 cm)
Edition of 3
Courtesy Margo Leavin Gallery,
Los Angeles

Fig. 34. (Right)
Edward Ruscha
(American, born 1937)
*Large Trademark with
Eight Spotlights,* 1962
Oil on canvas
66³/₄ x 133¹/₄ inches
(169.5 x 338.5 cm)
Whitney Museum of American Art,
Purchase, with funds from the
Mrs. Percy Uris Purchase Fund

double-entendres and thus inflected with a meaning both for those "in the know" as well as for all "outsiders," the language of camp has been channeled by Johnson into artworks spotlighting at last the experience of exclusion, alienation, and/or enforced dissembling. Though Johnson's form of address is usually gender-neutral, the unidentified characters in his "first person fictions"[152] clearly address us from a cool-headed and resolutely rooted gay standpoint.[153] *Untitled (Admit Nothing)* (fig. 33) is a case in point: the image of a stack of movie ticket reels, each ticket stamped with the barely legible phrase, "Admit My Ass," forces one to question to what extent homosexuality has (or, more accurately, has not) been admitted into the supposedly most democratic of public forums, the movies. Depending on one's phonetic emphasis[154] this phrase is simultaneously a plaintive cry for inclusion and a sarcastic, even angry comment on the homosexual's outsider status.

> let us walk in that nearby forest, staring into the growling trees
> in which an era of pompous frivolity or two is dangling its knobby knees
> and reaching for an audience
> —Frank O'Hara[155]

Larry Johnson's series of winter landscapes (see pls. 20, 22) are something like the visual equivalent of camp's fierce artifice and deliberate lack of depth, communicated here through an icy perfection of style. In *Winter Me*, for example, the words of a flamboyant and exasperated "star" take the form of a spoiled lament emblazoned drive-in-movie-screen size, across a long, flat, monochrome wedge, whose sharp diagonal thrust recalls the salient form in Ruscha's early trademark paintings (see fig. 34).[156] Though earlier Johnson works lift texts directly from talk show transcriptions, tabloid newspapers, and *People* magazine articles devoted to celebrity-dom, since 1988 the artist has composed his own "first person fic-

tions" which have been devised to retain, however, the thoroughly rehearsed confessional style in all of its whining extravagance of tabloid journalism.[157] The desolation of Johnson's barren snowscape and the jadedness saturating its billboard-size complaint are all the more jarring for being set within the normally cheerful context of a cartoon frame or cell. This work's visual evocation of mass entertainment production—of scripting, storyboarding, and animation—gives the lie that much more harshly to the far-from-innocent amusement industry. Johnson's focus here on the crisp, cold and finally brutal psychological "landscape" of the culture industry ties his art to a long West Coast literary tradition of Hollywood *noir*: a literature "focused on unmasking the 'bright, guilty place' ([Orson] Welles) called Los Angeles."[158]

> There was a desert wind blowing that night. It was one of those hot dry Santa Anas that come down through the mountain passes and curl your hair and make your nerves jump and your skin itch. On nights like that every booze party ends in a fight. Meek little wives feel the edge of the carving knife and study their husbands' necks. Anything can happen.
> —Raymond Chandler[159]

> Ordinarily, I detest narration, but the very fitting, realistically philosophical, poignantly cynical and, at times, hilarious words used to detail the queer coincidence which placed Jay, Abigail, and The Count in the path of death and destruction yet spared Jackie and Rex, Jerzy, Cary and many, many others, myself included, truthfully portrays, with very little dialogue, the haunting, frightening quality of this simply written, yet classically tragic story.
> —Larry Johnson[160]

In the tradition of Raymond Chandler, Nathanael West, and, later, Joan Didion, Johnson's narrative model combines "sunshine and *noir*"[161] in a voice that is stylized, ironically detached, and ulti-

mately cynical. Distinguished both by a literal clarity of presentation and an apparent lack of suggestive ambiguity, this voice—redolent of a smoothly stylized irony—is at once resistant to and aloofly inviting of interpretation. Johnson's narrative posture, like that of Tod Hackett in West's *Day of the Locust*, is one of both diffident removal, the watching "fascinatedly from somewhere on the sidelines,"[162] and of protectively self-concealing engagement: the recasting of all his sun-shot scenes under the harsher light of a moral chill.

> *I live in a place with acute linguistic and racial tensions.*
> *I use the city like a laboratory—its chemistry informs my work.*
> —Barbara Steinman[163]

In the province of Quebec, Montreal is the second largest city (after Paris) in the world having French as its official language, and the only major city in the American hemisphere that has granted French this linguistic distinction—a distinction that has rendered Montreal and the Quebec province minority geographies within English-speaking Canada. Language, as one of the badges of identity, is a hotly contested subject in Quebec; and it has not been uncommon for the individual's freedom of expression—or, more specifically, choice of tongue—to run into sharp conflict with the interests of citizens' groups bent on maintaining Quebec's Francophone character. A little over a decade ago, Quebec passed a law forbidding any outdoor signage that was not in French, and at the time of this writing the newly elected Québecois government has made the province's secession from Canada a very real possibility. This recent political development, coupled with Quebec's exclusionary linguistic laws, has helped buttress a hierarchy of power in Montreal that officially favors the French-speaking Catholic majority and marginalizes all other groups.

It is no wonder, then, that language should be a predominant element of **Barbara Steinman**'s work. Her environment's unique linguistic situation has attuned her not merely to the possibility of multiple languages, but also to the power—and to the effects of this power on the individual and the community—conferred on the speaker of a particular tongue. Unlike many word-oriented Conceptual artists whose explorations of language pivot on linguistic theory, Steinman's use of language always points to a specific sociopolitical context.[164] Steinman herself has stated, "I am interested in how people from varied cultural and linguistic backgrounds share the same territory in a place involved with nationalistic desires."[165]

In *Objects and Instruments* (plate 48 and inset), language appears etched over the faces of magnifying lenses set into brass tripods, each of which resembles a compass—an instrument for measuring distances, directions, and locations. Each of the magnifying lenses, given its tripod support, should thus work as an optical instrument for the framing and detailing of a specific location; yet Steinman's instruments do just the opposite. In every instance, the magnifying glass does not clarify but rather clouds the ground it hovers over, by inserting between us and its supposed point of focus the sentence "The Center of the World Is Exactly Where You Stand." Not only does language here literally obscure our vision, but the

flatly declarative sentence, multiplied at least a dozen times on the separate "instruments" placed throughout the installation, is itself both ironically subverted by and in turn subverts the unspoken principle that optical devices like the compass are designed to serve: that is, the single authoritative point of view and, by metaphorical extension, a single, indisputable, institutionalized authority.

"Milieu: *mille lieux*, a thousand places."[166] By directing our attention to the multiplicity of possible positions, each as valid as the next, Steinman disputes the notion of an incontestable center. She refuses to dictate for us a fixed point of view or, for that matter, viewing location, obliging us instead to circulate actively through her work in the gallery space. In order to see all the "instruments" comprising her installation, we must perambulate the gallery; in order to see into any one of her sculptures, we must bend slightly (but emphatically) at the waist. The normally passive act of looking is transformed into a highly conscious participatory event. *Objects and Instruments* itself thus provocatively embodies and enforces us bodily to experience "the concept that knowledge and meaning always shift, are never complete.... There is always another viewpoint. The difficulty in seeing all the elements at once is equivalent to the difficulty of placing or fixing meaning."[167]

Not only does Steinman mount a passionate if restrained critique of institutionalized authority, that "grand narrative [which] has lost its credibility, regardless of what mode of unification it uses";[168] she also underscores the importance of the individual and of the individual viewpoint (each one "the center of the world"), giving weight to the "interior, *non*geographic site"[169] of every man's or woman's identity. It matters not in the least if the individual in question is marginalized, as the photographic portion of *Objects and Instruments* subtly points out. Two large photographs have been hung by Steinman at the opposite far corners of the gallery's back wall, so that they call attention as much to the space separating them as to their very subject matter. In each photograph a female palm faces outward, its skin either emanating or reflecting light in a gesture reminiscent of thwarted prayer. Yet the hands, instead of beseeching, appear to push against the gallery's walls as if to make space for someone "outside"—for someone located at or beyond institutional edges, someone regularly denied any spot on the public stage. The palms betray a female body's presence and attempt to make way for it, although this body is apparent to us here only in a fragmentary form.

> *All immigrants and exiles know the peculiar restlessness of*
> *an imagination that can never again have faith in its own absolute-*
> *ness.... Because I have learned the relativity of cultural meanings*
> *on my skin, I can never take any one set of meanings as final. I*
> *doubt that I'll ever become an ideologue of any stripe; I doubt that*
> *I'll become an avid acolyte of any school of thought. I know that*
> *I've been written in a variety of languages.... It's not the worst*
> *place to live; it gives you an Archimedean leverage from which to*
> *see the world.*
> —Eva Hoffman[170]

Steinman's own acute awareness of her position as a Montreal outsider—and her consequent desire to undermine constructs of centered authority and to ensure both recognition and tolerance for a multiplicity of points of view—have undoubtedly been in part informed by her Jewish heritage. Inspired by her knowledge of a history of dispossession and exile spanning four millennia, Steinman offers in *Objects and Instruments* an imaginary geography which echoes the Jewish diaspora, an unfixed "place" or rather a condition that is always "making site of non-site."[171] *Objects and Instruments* speaks of a tenuous—but perhaps for that reason all the more poignantly hungry—relation to the concept of homeland; and it displays an acceptance of the nomadic condition for which identity is no longer a blind circumstance of place of birth or of native tongue but a consciously arrived at awareness of one's *relative* location or position in the world, a position no less integrally coherent for being relative.

Experience which is passed on from mouth to mouth is the source from which all storytellers have drawn. And among those who have written down the tales, it is the great ones whose written version differs least from the speech of the many nameless storytellers.

— *Walter Benjamin*[172]

I have been creating one-woman shows out of interviews. I do the interviews and then perform all of the interviewees. The resulting performance is meant to capture the personality of a place by attempting to embody its varied population and varied points of view in one person—myself. Often, the shows are built around a specific controversial and timely event or series of events.

— *Anna Deavere Smith*[173]

Actress, playwright, and performance artist **Anna Deavere Smith** bears witness in her works to one particular place and time: the United States in the 1980s and 1990s, on the eve of the millennium. Her solo performance series, *On the Road: A Search for American Character*, an ongoing chronicle not only performed but also conceived, developed, and written by Smith, has evolved since its inception in 1983 into more than a dozen anthology pieces derived from over 600 interviews she has herself conducted (see fig. 35). Each of the interview subjects chosen by Smith has been involved in an event having seminal bearing upon social developments such as intercultural relations, sexual politics, and black identity. *On the Road*, taking its parts together, represents Smith's exploration of the "American character" and the democratic experiment that is the United States.[174] Her material is language; her method, to study her taped interviews over and over "until I wear the words."[175] In performance, Smith reproduces with uncanny precision the many and often contradictory voices she has heard, including their accents and idiosyncratic cadences as well as the uncomfortable silences, mutterings, and ramblings that naturally accompany everyday speech. Smith also re-creates the unique physiognomic traits and bodily gestures or mannerisms belonging to the person whose voice and words have been recorded (fig. 36).[176] One after the next, Smith performs captivatingly exact portrayals of real individuals, expressing a vast range of emotions from rage, pain, and anxiety to sympathy, resignation, and acquiescence. Two

of her best-known works focus on moments of sheer crisis: *Fires in the Mirror: Crown Heights, Brooklyn and Other Identities* (the fourteenth *On the Road* piece) revolves around the conflicts that erupted in August 1991 between the Orthodox Jewish and African-American/Caribbean-American communities of Crown Heights, Brooklyn, while *Twilight: Los Angeles, 1992* (the fifteenth piece) retells the events of the 1992 Los Angeles uprising that followed the acquittal of four white police officers charged in the beating of a black man, Rodney King.

Fires in the Mirror is a collage of twenty-six characters fashioned from fifty interviews Smith conducted in Crown Heights, where Hassidic Jews and African Americans and Caribbean Americans, who, though living in close physical proximity to each other, are worlds apart in their customs and beliefs. On August 19, 1991, Gavin Cato, a seven-year-old Caribbean-American boy from the neighborhood, was killed and his cousin Angela seriously injured by a runaway car in the motorcade of the Rabbi Menachem Mendel Schneerson, the spiritual leader of the Lubavitcher Hassidim. For the following three days, the community was wracked by violent street demonstrations which led to, among other incidents, the retaliatory fatal stabbing of Yankel Rosenbaum, a twenty-nine-year-old Hassidic student. Smith, with an utterly even-handed compassion for the predicament of both sides, recounts in her performance this painful event through a host of discrepant, cacophonous, and even antagonistic voices, which by way of the artist's deft transcript editing and character juxtapositions on stage are made to interlock and communicate with each other—to form, in Smith's words, "the *illusion* of dialogue."[177] Words are balanced between the two groups in both power and cutting brevity when Smith matches her portrait of Minister Conrad Muhammad of the Nation of Islam, and his account of black slavery, with Letty Cottin Pogrebin, author of *Deborah, Golda and Me*, and her anecdote of how she learned of the Holocaust from an uncle. Moving from one character to another using a minimal change of props and costumes (donning in turn a yarmulke, a sweater, a wig, an African kente cloth) Smith allows for the uninterrupted airing of voices that range between the famous (or infamous) and the utterly unknown and mostly unheard.

Twilight: Los Angeles gives equal and eloquent voice to an even more complex human landscape of colliding ethnic groups (African Americans, Latinos, Asians, whites), all involved to some degree in the extreme civil disorder that followed in the wake of the April 29, 1992, jury verdict in the Rodney King beating case—the real-time image of the beating itself burned into public consciousness through the continuous televised replay of the amateur videotape on which it was captured. The collective portrait Smith projects of Los Angeles, the most racially and culturally diverse city in the United States and, for many, the paradigm for this nation's polyethnic future, is compelling and unsparing in its details and consequent emotional force. From two hundred and twenty interviews conducted over a period of eight months, Smith developed twenty-six portrayals of widely divergent individuals, each of her characters espousing a distinct and passionately heartfelt position. Among them: Reginald Denny, the white truck driver who suffered a heinous beating also caught on a video aired throughout the United States;

Elvira Evers, a pregnant Panamanian cashier who survived a random gunshot wound, her unborn baby clipped on its elbow by the stray bullet; Theodore Briseno, one of the four L.A.P.D. officers acquitted in King's beating; Angela King, Rodney King's aunt; Mrs. Young-Soon Han, a Korean liquor store owner whose business was looted; and Twilight Bey, a gang youth who negotiated a truce in 1992 between two of Los Angeles's most notorious and violent gangs, the Crips and the Bloods.[178] Finally, during the actual performance of *Twilight*, Smith exhibits excerpts from related TV footage, thus identifying the media itself as a critically powerful actor in the maelstrom of events—and an actor with its own strongly biased points of view. In contrast to the video sound-bites, however, Smith's work is constructed to resist relaying information quickly and tidily. Rather, her performance re-presents a series of individuals' groping efforts to give voice—or articulation—to and thereby understand the seemingly irrational human acts engendered by a crisis and the

anger and anguish inevitably accompanying them. Through everyday language we are taken by Smith's characters to a point at which emotions run so deep that we, along with our conductors, are at a loss for words to describe the experience.[179] This stoppage is the breakdown of syntax and readily coherent sense found at the heart of any profound emotional trauma. Yet, as Smith recognizes, it is the very inability to glibly give voice that may serve as a ground for the discovery of a new, more subtle, and more encompassing tongue.

In any one performance work, Smith's individual portraits gradually give way to a larger picture of the prevailing social forces and cultural constructs that have informed (and continue to inform) each of her characters' attitudes, views, and actions: forces that may be invisible to these characters themselves, but which through Smith's skillful distillation become as audible and visible to us as the human voices and faces the artist so precisely depicts. The forces to which Smith above all points are the history and current state of race relations in the United States; and the message Smith specifically conveys through her epic ventriloquism is the inadequacy of our language(s) to sustain a constructive dialogue about race. Was what happened in Crown Heights a "revolt" or a "pogrom?" Did Los Angeles experience an "uprising" or a "riot?" To agree on a single definition would require not merely a shared vocabulary, but more importantly, a common perspective. What Smith's works make irresistibly clear is the urgent need for a vocabulary and a vision that can more accurately assist us in facing, discussing, and understanding race issues.[180] In the words of Robert Sherman, as played by Smith, "We probably have 70 different kinds of [words for] bias, prejudice, racism, and discrimination, but it's not in our mind-set to be clear about it. So I think that we have sort of a *lousy language* on the subject, and that is a reflection of our unwillingness to deal with it honestly and to sort it out. I think we have a very, very *bad* language."[181] However inadequate, our vernacular speech is the linguistic instrument chosen by Smith from which to shape a "language for discussing difference"; and for her, "the only way we find that language is by talking *in* it—not *about* it—and talking in it in these moments of crisis, when our anxieties are so big that we can barely speak."[182] Smith's artistry lies in her first locating and then editing and carefully juxtaposing raw material,[183] and, when performing, in her uncanny ability to erase herself—she is usually barefoot, dressed neutrally in black slacks and white shirt—in order for her performance to cross more effortlessly boundaries of color, gender, age, race, religion, and social class.

The fugue of voices in Smith's *On The Road* heralds a new type of mapping or spatial visualization with which to cross the "racial frontier."[184] It sketches a course that has no fixed boundaries or foregone conclusions—one that is necessarily incomplete, fluid, and ever questing, because it lies precisely in that "zone of direct contact with developing reality"[185] in which (in 1995) "the cultural definition of the poly-ethnic [United States] of the year 2000 has

Fig. 35.
Anna Deavere Smith in South Central Los Angeles, February 1993

Fig. 36.
Anna Deavere Smith as use-of-force expert Sergeant Charles Duke in *Twilight: Los Angeles, 1992* at the Mark Taper Forum, June 13–July 18, 1993

barely begun."[186] Like the classic storyteller, Smith gives "counsel, less an answer to a question than a proposal concerning the continuation of a story which is just unfolding": a counsel which, when "woven into the fabric of real life... is wisdom."[187]

While creating a forum for a many-voiced dialogue founded on a common humanity, Smith's works continue to insist on the absolute individuality of their human characters. In a sense, her performances *positively* recover from the anonymity of day-to-day existence what had been only negatively dragged forward by a cataclysmic event: specific, isolated, and denominated individuals who in their very uniqueness the viewer comes to recognize as fundamentally akin to himself or herself. This empathy allows us to listen to the struggle of Smith's characters, which we must now address—a struggle by means of language to transform inculcated attitudes, or ideology, and to arrive at a rehabilitative understanding not only of events, but also of their human agents. Smith's interest lies not in achieving a unified or signature voice, but in highlighting a social— a "vocal"—complexity.[188] Her goal is to communicate both the essence of the individual *and* the essentially collective character of our place and age.[189] Returned by her works to the particulars of person and place and time (the former her cast of characters, the latter the late twentieth-century United States), we are given an opportunity by which to begin deciphering the deeper forces— legal, social, cultural, and personal—that govern our world. Smith, in baring these forces, is neither optimistic nor pessimistic about their future metamorphosis, but she is, and asks us to be, deeply engaged.

An individual cannot be completely incarnated into the flesh of existing sociohistorical categories. There is no mere form that would be able to incarnate once and forever all of his human possibilities and needs, no form in which he could exhaust himself down to the last word... no form that he could fill to the very brim and yet at the same time not splash over the brim. There always remains an unrealized surplus of humanness; there always remains a need for the future, and a place for this future must be found.
—*Mikhail Bakhtin*[190]

The artists in this exhibition build scenarios in their works that construct place and imagine, as well, its transformation. These works, and our experiences of them, are movements of creation, transgression, metamorphosis, and evolution. Affirming the individual— however contingent, however "constructed"—the works represented here ask that we be accountable to "place"—no matter how geographically flexible or fluid and discontinuous over time. Their authors create, so that we may experience, "a psychic sense of space,"[191] which, in its concentrated focus on the most important issues of our time, creates a vivid connection to the everyday world and a truthfulness to ongoing human experience. Each of the works in this exhibition composes an intensely poetic, generous, and new "geography" grounded in the human capacity for fantasy; a geography whose moral strength ultimately lies in the beauty that these works embody. That the artists and their works, as well as their works' viewers, are tied to place is precisely what enables the possibility of human intercession in fields at once personal, local, cultural, and beyond.

Notes

1. Hannah Arendt, *The Origins of Totalitarianism* (San Diego, New York, and London: Harcourt Brace Jovanovich, 1973). Also quoted in Barbara Steinman's sculpture *Cenotaph* (National Gallery of Canada, Ottawa).

2. For a profoundly original reading of the use of human bodily pain in the exercise of power, see Elaine Scarry, *The Body in Pain: The Making and Unmaking of the World* (New York: Oxford University Press, 1985), especially the introduction and the chapter "The Structure of Torture."

3. Charles Merewether, "Naming Violence in the Work of Doris Salcedo," *Third Text* 24 (1993), p. 43. This is a beautifully written treatise on Salcedo's work.

4. Ibid., p. 42.

5. bell hooks, *Yearning: Race, Gender, and Cultural Politics* (Boston: South End Press, 1990), p. 147.

6. Ann Hamilton, in Celia McGee, "A Certified 'Genius' Tangles with Horsehair," *The New York Times*, Oct. 3, 1993, sec. H, p. 41.

7. Ann Hamilton, in Chris Bruce, "The Revery of Labor," in Seattle, Henry Art Gallery, University of Washington, *Ann Hamilton: São Paulo/Seattle*, exh. cat. (1992), p. 32.

8. Ann Hamilton, in Kay Larson, exhibition review, *New York* (Nov. 1, 1993), p. 96.

9. Ann Hamilton, in Hugh M. Davies and Lynda Forsha, "A Conversation with Ann Hamilton," in La Jolla, San Diego Museum of Contemporary Art, *Ann Hamilton*, exh. cat. (1991), p. 64.

10. This artist's project was curated by Anne Rorimer.

11. William Cronin, *Nature's Metropolis: Chicago and the Great West* (New York and London: W.W. Norton, 1991), p. 72.

12. I borrow this term from the title of William Cronin's book (note 11).

13. Rodney Graham, in Jeff Wall, "Into the Forest," in Vancouver, Vancouver Art Gallery, *Rodney Graham*, exh. cat. (1988), p. 11.

14. Through quoting, forms of representation are "simultaneously acted out and criticized; [their] cultural-conventional roots are laid bare at the same moment that they exercise their effect on us." Thomas McEvilley, "On the Manner of Addressing Clouds," *Art and Discontent: Theory at the Millenium* (New York: McPherson and Company, 1991), p. 92.

15. Rodney Graham, in Ellen Ramsey, "Rodney Graham, James Welling," *Vanguard* (Feb./Mar. 1987), p. 33.

16. Jeff Wall, "Traditions and Counter-Traditions in Vancouver Art: A Deeper Background for Ken Lum's Work," *Witte de With: The 1990 Lectures* (Rotterdam: Witte de With Center for Contemporary Art, 1991), p. 68. "Commonwealth Romanticism," as defined by Wall, was easily transposed in postcolonial times to Canada's own nationalistic desires, which "gives up some of the impulses of the old overt colonial attitudes, but which continues them in a context of the new national aspirations of former colonies. Throughout all its phases, it continues the idea of the domestication of the frontier. Canada shares this idea, this myth, with the Americans." My observations on Rodney Graham's work are indebted to this essay.

17. "I don't think there could be a work which is more perfectly negative in relation to the lyrical landscape tradition. And yet, it continues this tradition in its negativity. It reinvents the tradition." Ibid., p. 79.

18. Robert Linsley, "Image Literatures," in Barcelona, Centre d'Art Santa Mònica, *Càmeres Indiscretes*, exh. cat. (1992), p. 112.

19. Wall (note 16), p. 110.

20. Ibid., p. 111.

21. Dan Graham and Robin Hurst, "Corporate Arcadias," in Dan Graham, *Rock My Religion: Writings and Art Projects, 1965–1990*, ed. Brian Wallis (Cambridge, Mass.: MIT Press, 1993), p. 275.

22. Andrea Zittel, in the gallery brochure for her exhibition at the Jack Hanley Gallery, San Francisco, Mar. 31–May 1, 1993.

23. Andrea Zittel, in the press release for her exhibition at the Andrea Rosen Gallery, New York, Sept. 10–Oct. 16, 1993.

24. The influence of Dan Graham on the work of Zittel's generation, not to mention on the work of Rodney Graham, Jeff Wall, and others, cannot be underestimated, for his writings and projects have proved crucial in the development of a socially critical conceptual art practice. Regarding Zittel's work, Graham's projects serve as precedents for cross-disciplinary models that are neither "pure" sculpture nor "pure" architecture/social experiment, but exist somewhere in between.

25. Dan Graham, "Homes for America," in *Rock My Religion* (note 21), pp. 14–23. The houses Dan Graham describes date from the end of World War II, when defense workers were situated in great numbers in Southern California, necessitating the speedy production of mass-produced houses.

26. Ibid.

27. For a study of the similarities between suburban architecture and modernist precepts, see Kathryn Hixson, "A Suburban Anthropology," in Chicago, Museum of Contemporary Art, *Radical Scavenger(s): The Conceptual Vernacular in Recent American Art*, exh. cat. by Richard Francis (1994), pp. 17–21.

28. Zittel (note 23). Zittel's interest in the modification of human behavior is an outgrowth of earlier projects devoted to conditioning not people, but animals such as houseflies and Bantam chickens. She built "breeding and management" units designed to manipulate the animals' behavior, which led her to apply organizational schemes to her own living environment: "The idea was to optimize my domestic life within given conditions." Zittel reconfigured her tiny apartment to accommodate all her activities as efficiently as possible. She was soon commissioned to create similar designs for other people's living spaces, marking the beginning of A–Z Administrative Services.

29. Andrea Zittel, in Valerie Filipovna, "Breeding as Art: Andrea Zittel Finds Truth in a Chicken," *Paper* (Summer 1993), unpag. copy.

30. Ibid.

31. John Brinckerhoff Jackson, *A Sense of Place, A Sense of Time* (New Haven: Yale University Press, 1994), p. viii.

32. Eugenio Dittborn, *Cahier #2* (Rotterdam: Witte de With Center for Contemporary Art, 1994), pp. 71–74.

33. Eugenio Dittborn, in Guy Brett, "Dust Clouds," *Mapa* (London, Institute of Contemporary Art, and Rotterdam, Witte de With Center for Contemporary Art, 1993), p. 76.

34. Interestingly, *Dulle Griet*, like Dittborn's own work, carries a hidden political commentary, for it is an allegorical indictment of the Spanish Occupation and its brutality against the Flemish people during Bruegel's time, disguised by the painter through the subject's reference to such popular sayings as "When you go to Hell, go sword in hand," or "He could plunder in front of hell and go unscathed." See Walter S. Gibson, *Bruegel* (New York and Toronto: Oxford University Press, 1977), p. 102 and *passim*.; and Robert L. Delevoy, *Bruegel*, trans. Stuart Gilbert (New York: Skira/Rizzoli International Publications, Inc., 1959), pp. 68–75.

35. Roberto Merino, "Signs of Travel: A Conversation between Roberto Merino and Eugenio Dittborn," in *Mapa* (note 33), p. 10.

36. Ibid., p. 7.

37. Dittborn welcomes the folds in his fabric surfaces as the traits of a typical letter and as an important compositional device, for the folds generate a grid system within which Dittborn deploys his imagery. In this way, "Airmail Paintings travel through the international postal network as *folded* letters and are shown at their destinations as *unfolded* paintings." Eugenio Dittborn, "Roadrunner," *Third Text* (Winter 1990/91), n. pag.

38. Guy Brett, "Open only on Conditions Specified," in Sean Cubitt and Guy Brett, *Camino Way*, ed. Eugenio Dittborn (Santiago de Chile, 1991).

39. New York, The Museum of Modern Art, *Sense and Sensibility: Women Artists and Minimalism in the Nineties*, exh. cat. by Lynn Zelevansky (1994), p. 22. See also Amada Cruz, "Jac Leirner," in Washington D.C., Hirshhorn Museum and Sculpture Garden, Smithsonian Institution, *Directions*, exh. brochure (1993).

40. Jac Leirner, in Guy Brett, "A Bill of Wrongs," in São Paulo, Galeria Millan, *Jac Leirner*, exh. cat. (1989), n. pag. See also Alma Guillermoprieto, "Obsessed in Rio," *The New Yorker* (Aug. 16, 1993), pp. 44–55.

41. It should be said that steps are being taken to stabilize the Brazilian economy, including the establishment of a new currency, the *real*.

42. *Monte Carlo Bond* used the readymade and institutionalized chance-based structure of the casino roulette wheel for an artwork in which Duchamp usurped the casino's rules of operation. See David Joselit, "Marcel Duchamp's *Monte Carlo Bond Machine,*" *October* (Summer 1992), pp. 8–26.

43. Warhol's serial reproductions of dollar bills—ubiquitous icons of the everyday world along with Campbell's soup cans—were some of the first subjects produced by the artist using the silkscreening technique that became key to his art.

44. Vladimir Herzog was a journalist whose death in the early 1970s at the hands of the police caused a national scandal in Brazil. See *Sense and Sensibility* (note 39), p. 24. See also Paulo Herkenhoff, "Deconstructing the Opacities of History," in Austin, Texas, Archer M. Huntington Library, The University of Texas at Austin, *Encounters/Displacements: Luis Camnitzer, Alfredo Jaar, Cildo Meireles,* exh. cat. by Mari Carmen Ramírez (1992). Meireles's contemporary Waltércio Caldas also created artworks using Brazilian currency during this period, and has likewise influenced Leirner's art.

45. This term is Carl Andre's.

46. Neo-Concretism, a movement founded in Rio de Janeiro in 1959 and active through the 1960s, was part of an international movement that advocated cultural freedom, innovation, and experimentation.

47. For example, many of Hélio Oiticica's unpretentious works were made to be worn in the public arena and carried with them a political dimension. See Paris, Galerie Nationale du Jeu de Paume; Rio de Janeiro, Projeto Hélio Oiticica; and Rotterdam, Witte de With Center for Contemporary Art, *Hélio Oiticica,* exh. cat. by Guy Brett, Catherine David, Chris Dercon, Luciano Figueiredo, and Lygia Pape (1992).

48. *The Random House Dictionary of the English Language: The Unabridged Edition* (New York: Random House, 1969).

49. *Traveller's Folding Item* is the title of a 1916 readymade by Duchamp consisting simply of an Underwood typewriter cover.

50. Simone Weil, quoted in Edward Said, "Reflections on Exile," *Granta* 13 (1984), p. 169.

51. Guillermo Kuitca, interviewed by Lydia Dona, *Journal of Contemporary Art* (Summer 1993), p. 56.

52. Alicia Duvojne Ortiz, quoted in James Clifford, *The Predicament of Culture* (Cambridge, Mass.: Harvard University Press, 1988), p. 185. Ortiz is a Jewish Argentinian writer living in Paris.

53. Charles Merewether, "Between Time, Between Places: The Passage of Desire in the Paintings of Kuitca," in Rome, Gian Enzo Sperone, *Guillermo Kuitca,* exh. cat. (1990), n. pag.

54. Ibid.

55. Charles Merewether, "Displacement and the Reinvention of Identity," in New York, The Museum of Modern Art, *Latin American Artists of the Twentieth Century,* exh. cat., ed. Waldo Rasmussen, with Fatima Bercht and Elizabeth Ferrer (1993), p. 152. Democracy was restored to Argentina in 1983 when a constitutional government took power from a military regime following the Falkland wars of 1982.

56. Prudence Carlson, unpublished manuscript.

57. Guillermo Kuitca, in Marcelo E. Pacheco, "Guillermo Kuitca: A Painter's Inventory," in *A Book Based on Guillermo Kuitca* (Amsterdam: Contemporary Art Foundation, 1993), p. 182. Here Kuitca is referring to the work of Pina Bausch, by whom he was deeply influenced when her Wuppertal Dance Theater performed in Buenos Aires in 1980; so inspired was Kuitca by Bausch's work that he became a theater director and in 1984 produced *El Mar Dulce [The Sweet Sea],* whose subject concerned the immigrant populations who arrived in Argentina by way of the Rio de la Plata.

58. Regarding the series of paintings based on real and imaginary genealogical charts entitled *People on Fire,* the artist has said, "My work is about those persons not having a background, about a name without a background." Guillermo Kuitca, interviewed by Josefina Ayerza, in "Guillermo Kuitca: On the Map," *Flash Art* (Nov./Dec. 1993), p. 46.

59. Merewether (note 55), p. 145; Merewether explained: "The cultural and social histories of Latin American nations remind us that the formation of identity...has developed through historical processes of displacement, dispossession, and fragmentation....[o]riginating during the Conquest, when European colonizers appropriated the lands of indigenous communities and subsequently tried to eradicate native cultures, languages, and religions" (p. 144).

60. Henri Foucault has described the cemetery as "the 'other' city, where each family possesses its dark resting place"; see Henri Foucault, "Of Other Spaces," *Diacritics* 16 (1986), p. 25.

61. Carlson (note 56).

62. Henri Foucault described heterotopias as places "formed in the very founding of society—which are something like counter-sites, a kind of effectively enacted utopia in which the real sites, all the other real sites that can be found within the culture, are simultaneously represented, contested, and inverted. Places of this kind are outside of all places, even though it may be possible to indicate their location in reality." Each heterotopia "has a precise and determined function within a society": among other heterotopias, Foucault has enumerated the fair ground, the rest home, the psychiatric hospital, and the museum and library ("heterotopias of indefinitely accumulating time"). The role of the heterotopia is "to create a space that is other, another real space, as perfect, as meticulous, as well arranged as ours is messy, ill constructed, and jumbled." As a preeminent heterotopic example, Foucault turned to the cemetery: "The cemetery is certainly a place unlike ordinary cultural spaces. It is a space that is however connected with all the sites of the citystate or society or village, etc., since each individual, each family has relatives in the cemetery"; see Foucault (note 60), pp. 22–27.

63. Michel Foucault, describing Borges's writing, which served as an inspiration for his own book *The Order of Things.* See Brian Wallis, "Introduction," in New York, The New Museum of Contemporary Art, *Art After Modernism: Rethinking Representation* (Boston: David R. Godine, 1984), p. xiv.

64. Clifford (note 52), p. 173.

65. Since 1569, the map most often used to describe the world, and thus determining our vision of it, has been the Mercator, created to abet European navigators in their discovery and colonization of non-Western climes. By virtue of its long use and institutional authority, this instrument continues to reinforce a world view that places Europe at the world center—in all ways including geographic. One cartographic response to the Mercator's biases and distortions is the Peters map, first published in 1974, which represents all areas of the world according to relative size.

66. Mari Carmen Ramírez, "Introduction," in *El Taller Torres-García: The School of the South and Its Legacy* (Austin: University of Texas Press, 1992), p.3. This is an impressive in-depth study of Joaquín Torres-García's influence on modern art in Latin America and beyond.

67. In the European partitioning of the Americas, "the very lines on the map had been imposed on the continent with little reference to indigenous peoples, and indeed in many places with little reference to the land itself. The invaders parceled the continent among themselves in designs reflective of their own complex rivalries and relative power." See J. B. Harley, "Maps, Knowledge, and Power," in *The Iconography of Landscape* (Cambridge: Cambridge University Press, 1988), p. 282. See also Merewether (note 53).

68. "Surveyors marched alongside soldiers, initially mapping for reconaissance, then for general information, and eventually as a tool of pacification, civilization and exploitation in the defined colonies....Maps were used to legitimize the reality of conquest and empire. They helped create myths...communicat[e] an imperial message...[and] more than often acquired the force of law in the landscape." Ibid., pp. 282–83.

69. Think of these studs as starlike impressions evoking astronomical charts, yet another system by which we navigate the unknown.

70. Guillermo Kuitca, in Magalí Arriola, "Guillermo Kuitca," *Poliester* (Fall 1993), p. 36.

71. Clifford (note 52), p. 9.

72. James Joyce, *A Portrait of the Artist as a Young Man* (New York: Penguin Books, 1976), pp. 15–16. My thanks to Prudence Carlson for pointing this text out to me, and for contributing to an extraordinary extent towards this entry on Vija Celmins.

73. Johns, who was himself indebted to Magritte's work, was to extend this literalism to *objects* incorporated into his paintings.

74. Vija Celmins, in Amy Gerstler, "Vija Celmins," *Art Issues* (Nov. 1990).

75. Again, a similar deceleration has been perceptively noted in Jasper Johns' early paintings and sculptures. See Leo Steinberg, "Jasper Johns's: The First Seven Years of His Art," *Other Criteria* (New York: Oxford University Press, 1972), p. 29.

76. Vija Celmins, in Sheena Wagstaff, "Vija Celmins," *Parkett* (June 1992), p. 11. Wagstaff rightly points to Celmins's background as a determining factor in her development as an artist. Born in Latvia, Celmins migrated to Indianapolis as a child

refugee of World War II; subsequently she "further displaced herself from her origins by moving to California to complete her studies in the late '60s....for Vija Celmins the sense of displacement is a poignant one. 'Latvia will always by my first home [says Celmins]. That's where I was born. In another way the studio is a home because that's where everything happens for me. Czeslaw Milosz said it more eloquently: "Imagination can fashion a homeland." That statement is more than true for me.'"

77. Walt Whitman, "Preface to the Reader in the British Islands," *Specimen Days* (Boston: David R. Godine, 1971), p. I.

78. Said (note 50), p. 162.

79. Alfred Kazan, "Introduction," in *Specimen Days* (note 77), p. xix.

80. "I ask the public to help me, to take responsibility, to become part of my work, to join in." Felix Gonzalez-Torres, interviewed by Tim Rollins, in *Felix Gonzalez-Torres* (Los Angeles: A.R.T. Press, 1993), p. 23.

81. Felix Gonzalez-Torres, artist's statement for his exhibition at the Andrea Rosen Gallery, New York, 1990.

82. Felix Gonzalez-Torres, interviewed by Tim Rollins (note 80), p. 13.

83. "Of our communal mourning, perhaps only the Names Project quilt displays something of the psychic work of mourning...." Douglas Crimp, "Mourning and Militancy," *Out There: Marginalization and Contemporary Culture,* ed. Russell Ferguson, Martha Gever, Trinh T. Minh-ha, Cornel West (New York: The New Museum of Contemporary Art and MIT Press, 1990), p. 236. See also Simon Watney, "In Purgatory: The Work of Felix Gonzalez-Torres," *Parkett* 39 (1994), pp. 38–44.

84. Eric Troncy, "Felix Gonzalez-Torres: Placebo," *Art Press* (June 1993), p. 334.

85. hooks (note 5), pp. 42–43.

86. In conversation with the author, Marshall has stated that the title *Many Mansions* is a reference to a biblical phrase in which Jesus, referring to heaven, says "in my father's house there are many mansions." In his painting Marshall adapted the phrase to read "in my mother's house." He remembers hearing the phrase as a familiar refrain in his childhood.

87. Cornel West, "The New Cultural Politics of Difference," in *Out There* (note 83), p. 31.

88. Ibid., p. 34.

89. Amsterdam, Van Gogh Museum, *Pierre Puvis de Chavannes,* exh. cat. by Aimée Brown Price (1994), p. 14.

90. Ibid., p. 21.

91. This particular detail is a holdover from the days when Marshall wished to be a children's book illustrator.

92. Dan Graham, in Brian Wallis, "Introduction: Dan Graham's History Lessons," in *Rock My Religion* (note 21), p. xvi.

93. Kerry James Marshall, in Chicago, Spertus Museum, *Bridges and Boundaries: Chicago Crossings,* exh. cat. (1994), p. 21.

94. Teshome H. Gabriel, "Thoughts on Nomadic Aesthetics and Black Independent Cinema: Traces of a Journey," in *Out There* (note 83), p. 402.

95. *Daughters of the Dust* was directed by Julie Dash in 1991. *Sankofa* was directed by Haile Gerima in 1993.

96. Gabriel (note 94), p. 407.

97. West (note 87), p. 36.

98. "I see my work in photography as occupying a sort of interspace which never settles on any one medium." Jeff Wall, in Bill Jones, "False Documents: A Conversation with Jeff Wall," *Arts* (May 1990), p. 53.

99. "The opportunity is both to recuperate the past—the great art of the museums—and at the same time to participate with a critical effect in the most up-to-date spectacularity." Jeff Wall, interviewed by Els Barents, in *Jeff Wall: Transparencies* (New York: Rizzoli International Publications, Inc., 1987), 100.

100. Charles Baudelaire, "The Painter of Modern Life," in Jonathan Mayne, ed., *Charles Baudelaire, The Painter of Modern Life and Other Essays* (New York: Phaidon Press, 1964), pp. 12 and 40.

101. It is of no small significance that Wall studied at the Courtauld Institute in London in the 1970s when social art history was beginning to adopt a Marxist-influenced critique of nineteenth-century French painting. Wall's art of social criticism has been more *concurrent* with (if not in advance of) than influenced by the developments of academic art history. See Thomas Crow, "Profane Illuminations: Social History and the Art of Jeff Wall," *Artforum* (Feb. 1993), pp. 63–69.

102. Wall (note 16), p. 77.

103. Jeff Wall describes his project as "a program of *critical realism,* a kind of *painting of modern life,* carried out in a dialectically removed relationship to painting by means of its replacement with photography. In this development, modern pictorial art is understood as a continuous tradition." Ibid.

104. "...the speciality of the city experience in modern art is that most of this city experience has been in the capital cities—Berlin, Paris, or New York. That's been the main tradition.... In the 20th century, however, there has been a shift, where important historical experiences are now had in the secondary cities.... So a secondary city like Vancouver [or Tijuana] is now having a crucial historical experience." Wall, in Jones (note 98), p. 54.

105. See Julia Sagraves, "The Street," in Chicago, The Art Institute of Chicago, *Gustave Caillebotte: Urban Impressionist,* exh. cat. (1995), especially pp. 88 and 95.

106. Ian Wallace, "Jeff Wall's Transparencies," in London, Institute of Contemporary Art, *Jeff Wall: Transparencies,* exh. cat. (1984), n. pag.

107. Earl Shorris, "Raids, Racism, and the INS," *The Nation* (May 8, 1989), p. 682: a migration which has brought countless people (primarily from Central and South America since 1982) to the United States/Mexico border, to settle in towns and cities like the one pictured here: in neighborhoods barely old and by no means moneyed enough to have secured well-paved roads or decent permanent housing.

108. Jeff Wall in T. J. Clark, Serge Guilbaut, and Anne Wagner, "Representation, Suspicions, and Critical Transparency: An Interview with Jeff Wall," *Parachute* (July/Aug./Sept. 1990), p. 6.

109. Like Wall after him, Manet himself often based his compositions, if not his subject matter, on older works: in this case, on the tradition of the beggar-philosopher which was commonplace in seventeenth-century Spain, and the composition of Velázquez's *Menippus,* which Manet would have seen in the Museo del Prado. See Philadelphia Museum of Art and The Art Institute of Chicago, *Édouard Manet, 1832–1883,* exh. cat. by Anne Coffin Hanson (1966), pp. 45 and 93–95.

110. Jeff Wall, in Jones (note 98), p. 55.

111. Jeff Wall, in *Jeff Wall: Transparencies* (note 99), p. 103.

112. Jonathan Mayne, in *Charles Baudelaire* (note 100), p. xiii.

113. Roland Barthes, interview with Raymond Bellour, "On the Fashion System and the Structural Analysis of Narrative" (1967), trans. Linda Coverdale; reprinted in *The Grain of the Voice* (New York: Hill and Wang, 1985), pp. 50–51.

114. John Yau, "Words for and from Brice Marden," in Boston, Museum of Fine Arts, *Brice Marden: Boston,* exh. cat. by Trevor Fairbrother (1991), p. 25. The literature on Brice Marden is extensive; I am, however, particularly indebted to the writings of Klaus Kertess, Brenda Richardson, Yve-Alain Bois, and John Yau.

115. Brice Marden, in John Yau, "Brice Marden," *Flash Art* (Oct. 1988), p. 92. Brenda Richardson reported that when working in the studio, "the artist... thinks very much 'about natural objects turning into, and not quite turning into, abstractions.'" Brice Marden, in Brenda Richardson, *Brice Marden: Cold Mountain* (Houston: Houston Fine Art Press, 1992), p. 57.

116. Carlson (note 56).

117. Brice Marden, in Yve-Alain Bois, "Marden's Doubt," in Bern, Switzerland, Kunsthalle Bern, *Brice Marden: Paintings 1985–1993,* exh. cat. (1993), p. 53. It is by now well known, for example, that in 1966–67 Marden based his *Back Series* on the dimensions of the body of his wife, Helen.

118. Klaus Kertess, *Brice Marden: Paintings and Drawings* (New York: Harry N. Abrams, 1992), p. 45. Richardson's graceful description of the making of Marden's *Cold Mountain* series applies here as well: "Methodically, with tiny, sharp-edged palette knives, he scraped away the pigment from every stroke he brushed on the canvas. Lines became transparent, and in contradiction of logic, the paintings

seemed to resolve on the place, cohere, and grow less layered as their webs of drawn paint became more abundant. Despite layers and layers of oil...the constant scraping and sanding left the canvas exposed and eloquently raw, with a textural ground something like—and yet not like—abraded paper or ancient rock"; see Richardson (note 115), p. 67.

119. "Marden variously describes this covering over or scrubbing away of applied paint as 'erasures,' 'cancellations'...or simply 'corrections.'" Ibid., p. 69.

120. Richardson (note 115), p. 69. She continued: "When applied marks are 'erased' with solvent, the artist controls the degree to which the black lines mutate and dissolve into the painting's ground color."

121. In an interview with artist Pat Steir, Marden elaborated on his technique: "What happens in the paintings is I'll paint, then I'll paint things out, make corrections by painting out with white paint. I started doing that in the drawings, what happened was that what was painted out also became a positive image. It was sort of like a ghost image....everything there is there. The paintings, in a funny way, are very realistic, because there's no way I can take anything out. The things that get painted out suddenly become images on their own. I erase...but then that starts becoming an image itself." Brice Marden, in Pat Steir, "Brice Marden: An Interview," in New York, Matthew Marks Gallery, Brice Marden: Recent Drawings and Etchings, exh. cat. (1991), n. pag.

122. Bois (note 117), p. 35.

123. Ibid.

124. John Yau, "A Vision of the Unsayable," in London, Anthony d'Offay Gallery, Brice Marden: Recent Paintings and Drawings, exh. cat. (1988), sec. 4, n. pag.

125. For example, Marden's description of Pollock's painting technique echoes his own: "You look at the colors and the marks, and you try to redraw them. You look at the blacks and you follow the way they went on to the canvas, then you follow the whites, say, then the browns....But there's always some point where you lose the trail; you just can't read it because it never reads like layering...there are places where the black is over the white, and then there are places where the white is over the black. I don't really know how he was working those colors, how he could go back and forth between colors and layers. The colors may look layered, but I think there was a more organic flow between what looks like the bottom layer and what looks like the top layer. There just seems to be so much more: Pollock doesn't let the painting read as layers, and all those marks and colors become the real space of the painting." Brice Marden, in Richardson (note 115), p. 43. Marden's relationship to Pollock extends to an awareness of the former's involvement in the environment and traditional aesthetic vocabulary of the New York School: "I have a certain identification with the light in New York, which I think is in my painting. And I have a real identification with New York itself and everything about New York and about the tradition, albeit a very recent one, of New York painting. I know all of that is in me and in my painting" (p. 79).

126. Earning a living as a guard at the Jewish Museum in New York, Marden had the opportunity to study Johns's work in depth when Johns's retrospective was organized there in 1964. See Kertess (note 118), p. 13.

127. Carlson (note 56).

128. Ibid.

129. Jim Lewis, "Gerhard Richter: Betty," Artforum (Sept. 1993), p. 133.

130. Yve-Alain Bois, Painting as Model (Cambridge, Mass.: MIT Press, 1990), p. 250.

131. Marden acknowledges that these paintings reflect his physical make-up: "I am 5' 8½", and I weigh this much, and I am left-handed, and I'm a certain age. That has a big affect on what the thing looks like. The kind of mark I can make physically"; see Steir (note 121). Marden likes to work with long-handled brushes held at arm's length, a method that underscores his every movement and gesture.

132. Bois (note 117), p. 13.

133. Yau (note 124), sec. 14, n. pag.

134. Bois (note 117), p. 53.

135. Yau (note 124), sec. 14, n. pag.

136. Leonardo Drew, interviewed by Tim Nye, in New York, Thread Waxing Space, Leonardo Drew, exh. cat., essay by Thomas McEvilley (1992), p. 7.

137. Thomas McEvilley, "Leonardo Drew," in Ibid., pp. 13–14. McEvilley continued: "The years of gathering cast-off materials have left a mark on Drew's work that parallels to some extent the tradition of the southern African-American bricoleur."

138. Rosalind E. Krauss, The Optical Unconscious (Cambridge, Mass.: MIT Press, 1993), p. 248.

139. Rosalind E. Krauss, discussing Jackson Pollock's 1947 painting Full Fathom Five. Ibid., p. 293.

140. In speaking about the American postminimalist generation of artists, Richard Armstrong has succinctly stated that "for many, process connoted a wholesale adoption of gesture into sculpture." See Richard Armstrong, "Between Geometry and Gesture," in New York, Whitney Museum of American Art, The New Sculpture 1965–75: Between Geometry and Gesture, exh. cat., ed. Richard Armstrong and Richard Marshall (1990), p. 12.

141. McEvilley (note 137), p. 15.

142. Armstrong (note 140), p. 14.

143. McEvilley (note 137), p. 11.

144. Carlson (note 56).

145. Dave Hickey, "The Murmur of Eloquence: Intimations of the Full World," Los Angeles, Otis Gallery, Otis College of Art and Design, Plane/Structures, exh. cat. by David Pagel (1994), p. 29. Hickey is referring to Wallace Stevens's poem "Description without Place."

146. See Yve-Alain Bois, "Thermometers Should Last Forever," Edward Ruscha: Romance with Liquids/Paintings 1966–1969 (New York: Rizzoli International and Gagosian Gallery, 1993).

147. Bois has noted Ruscha's relationship to Abstract Expressionism: "Ruscha's liquid words are engaged in a dialogue with Pollock's drip paintings (note that they appear the same year as Pollock's major retrospective at the Museum of Modern Art, 1967), a dialogue," Bois adds, "that should not be too swiftly read as governed by irony." Bois also points to the Surrealist Salvador Dalí's pristine trompe l'oeil renditions of melting objects (such as watches) as forerunners of Ruscha's liquid works. Ibid., esp. pp. 27–31.

148. "L. A. is probably the most mediated town in America, nearly unviewable save through the fictive scrim of its mythologizers." Michael Sorkin, "Explaining Los Angeles," California Counterpoint: New West Coast Architecture 1982 (San Francisco: Institute for Architecture and Urban Studies and Rizzoli International), p. 8.

149. Christopher Isherwood, A Single Man (New York: Simon and Schuster, 1964), p. 35.

150. Susan Sontag, "Notes on Camp," A Susan Sontag Reader (New York: Vintage Books, 1983), pp. 105–19.

151. "Camp contains an explicit commentary on feats of survival in a world dominated by the taste, interests, and definitions of others." Andrew Ross, quoted in Terry R. Myers, "The Sincerely Fraudulent Photographs of Larry Johnson," Arts (Summer 1991), p. 41.

152. "I am the author of first person fictions." Larry Johnson, in David Rimanelli, "Larry Johnson: Highlights of Concentrated Camp," Flash Art (Nov./Dec. 1990), p. 122.

153. "One of the ways I would like to see my work functioning as 'of interest to gays' is as camp. Camp is an area in which I can claim ownership." Larry Johnson, in Rimanelli (note 152), p. 123.

154. That is, "admit my ass" or "admit, my ass." Again, Edward Ruscha provides a precedent for Johnson's sly phonetic game-playing: see, for example, Ruscha's word-and-image painting Big Men Run in My Family, which could also be read as "Big Men Run in My Family."

155. Frank O'Hara, "Ode on Causality," The Selected Poems of Frank O'Hara, ed. Donald Allen (New York: Alfred A. Knopf, 1974), pp. 135–36. It is particularly telling that for the text to Standing Still & Walking in Los Angeles Johnson should have reworked this Frank O'Hara poem, in which the line "standing still and walking in New York" appears. O'Hara, whose poems, critical writings, and curatorial essays embraced among many varied art forms the works of the Abstract Expressionists Robert Motherwell, Barnett Newman, Jackson Pollock, and Willem de Kooning, is also a touchstone figure within contemporary gay culture. From a conversation with Larry Johnson, Dec. 1994.

156. Johnson took the book *Zsa Zsa Gabor: My Life Story Written for Me by Gerald Frank* as inspiration for his own text.

157. "What I focus on are...the confession, the self-explanation, the release, the testimonial, the testimony. The things that have come to signify what is meaningful" when, in fact, "here emotion seems absent or misplaced...." Larry Johnson, in Rimanelli (note 152), p. 123.

158. Mike Davis, *City of Quartz* (New York: Vintage Books, 1992), p. 18. According to Mike Davis, "Hollywood *noir*" begins in 1934 with James M. Cain's *The Postman Always Rings Twice*, followed by "a succession of looking-through-the-hour-glass-darkly novels—all produced by writers under contract to the studio system—[that] repainted the image of Los Angeles as an urban hell...a regional fiction obsessively concerned with puncturing the bloated image of Southern California as the golden land of opportunity and the fresh start." Davis's phrase, the "Disneyification of *noir*," is perfectly suited to Johnson's work. See the chapter "Sunshine or Noir?" esp. pp. 38 and 46.

159. Raymond Chandler, "Red Wind," in *The Simple Art of Murder* (New York: W. W. Norton, 1968), p. 333.

160. Larry Johnson, text to "Classically Tragic Story."

161. Davis (note 158), p. 23.

162. Sorkin (note 148), p. 13.

163. Barbara Steinman, in New York, The New Museum of Contemporary Art, *Rhetorical Image*, exh. cat., ed. Milena Kalinovska and Deidre Summerbell (1990), n. pag.

164. This is not to deny a strong body of politically oriented, language-based art beyond that of Steinman's; nor is it to ignore the importance of that aspect of Conceptual art which addresses itself to an institutional critique of language per se and of systems of communications generally.

165. Barbara Steinman, unpublished artist's statement sent to author, 1994.

166. Edmond Jabès, *The Book of Margins*, trans. Marjorie Waldrop (Chicago: University of Chicago Press, 1993), p. 15. Steinman is an avid reader of Jabès, a Jewish philosopher of Egyptian origin who was born in Cairo in 1912 and lived in France from 1956 until his death in 1991. Jabès's writing style—typically enigmatic, combining aphorisms, prose meditation, and poetry—holds a special appeal for Steinman, who likewise prefers an indirect and evocative form of address.

167. Reesa Greenberg, "Barbara Steinman and *A Lapse in Logic*," in Windsor, Ontario, Art Gallery of Windsor, *Barbara Steinman: A Lapse in Logic*, exh. cat. (1994), p. 15.

168. Jean-Francois Lyotard, *The Postmodern Condition: A Report on Knowledge*, trans. Geoff Bennington and Brian Massuumi (Minneapolis: University of Minnesota Press, 1984).

169. Mary Jane Jacob, "Artists' Installations," in *Places with a Past: New Site-Specific Art at Charleston's Spoleto Festival* (New York: Rizzoli International, 1991), p. 59 [italics added].

170. Eva Hoffman, *Lost in Translation: A Life in a New Language* (New York: Penguin Books, 1989), p. 275. My thanks to Fred Henry for introducing me to this book.

171. Barbara Steinman, *Echoes of Earlier Appearances: Installation Works by Barbara Steinman* (Montreal: Galerie René Blouin, 1990), n. pag.

172. Walter Benjamin, "The Storyteller," *Illuminations*, with an intro. by Hannah Arendt (New York: Harcourt, Brace and World, 1968), p. 84.

173. Anna Deavere Smith, artist's statement accompanying her performances.

174. "I'm interested in capturing the American character through documenting... differences." Anna Deavere Smith, in Simi Horwitz, "About Face," *Theater Week* (June 22, 1992), p. 25.

175. Anna Deavere Smith, in Mary Talbot, "'Twilight's Best Gleaning," *New York Daily News*, Mar. 23, 1994, p. 36.

176. Smith differentiates her enterprise from that of mimicry or impersonation, both of which tend to exaggerate or caricature a person's most obvious characteristics. Rather than dramatizing her characters, Smith has explained, "I call myself a repeater....Or a reiterator, rather than a mimic." Anna Deavere Smith, in Richard Stayton, "The Voices of the City," *Los Angeles Times*, Apr. 25, 1993; Calendar section, p. 7.

177. Anna Deavere Smith, in Michael P. Scasserra, "A Jury of One," *Theater Week* (Mar. 28, 1994), p. 19 [italics added].

178. "My show is named *Twilight*. Partly it is because I was so taken by the young Crip who is working on the truce. His *nom de guerre* is Twilight. Also the upheaval took place at twilight. Twilight is a time when objects are obscured by the coming darkness. It is the time when we're not sure of whether it's dark or light. It's limbo time. It's quiet, it's not peace....It is a creative time because it asks more of our vision. We have to work harder to see....Our effort, our participation discerns reality...." Anna Deavere Smith, "A Fire in a Crowded Theatre: Anna Deavere Smith Relives the Los Angeles Riots: An Interview by Richard Stayton," *American Theater* (Jul./Aug. 1993), p. 23.

179. "What I'm really interested in is the very place where language fails. That's what interests me in my search for American character." Smith in Talbot (note 175), p. 37.

180. "For a little while we had words and images that made us think we could work things out. Like the idea of the melting pot, or the notion of integration. But we're in a funny time now. We don't have any words or pictures that we believe in.... We don't have the vocabulary to talk about [race]. Every day, our vocabulary seems more and more inadequate." Anna Deavere Smith, in Mervyn Rothstein, "Racial Turmoil in America: Tales from a Woman Who Listened," *The New York Times*, July 5, 1992.

181. At the time of the Brooklyn incidents, Robert Sherman was Director of the Community Relations Institute of the New York City Commission on Human Rights, and is played by Smith in *Fires in the Mirror*. His words are reproduced by Smith in "Defining Identity: Four Voices," *The New York Times*, Op-Ed Section, May 24, 1992. The very language in which issues of race are addressed is also discussed by Smith in the person of Angela Davis in *Fires in the Mirror*.

182. Stayton (note 176).

183. "My voice," she has stated, "is in the juxtaposition of other voices. It's in the choices that I make." Anna Deavere Smith, in Jack Kroll, "A Woman for all Seasons," *Newsweek* (June 1, 1992), p. 74.

184. "We don't have adequate language to discuss race right now. That's the frontier. How can we speak to one another and have it be meaningful—that's the challenge." Anna Deavere Smith, in Chris H. Smith, "Anna Deavere Smith Plays with Fire," *Artz* (August 1992), p. 39.

185. M. M. Bakhtin, "Epic and Novel," *The Dialogic Imagination: Four Essays*, trans. Caryl Emerson and Michael Holquist, ed. Michael Holquist (Austin: University of Texas Press, 1981), p. 39.

186. Davis (note 158), p. 24.

187. Benjamin (note 172), pp. 85–86. Smith has defined her work as "an unfinished message, the beginning of a dialogue, a provocation." See Scasserra (note 177), p. 27.

188. "What I'm offering...is a kind of an aggressive response to the damage the search for sameness has done for us." Anna Deavere Smith, in Jonathan Lahr, "Under the Skin," *The New Yorker* (June 28, 1993), p. 93.

189. "I am advocating for the individuality and diversity in our society....I am hoping to use theater as a place for creating community." Anna Deavere Smith, in Stephen Foehr, "Dousing Fires," *Chicago Tribune*, Dec. 26, 1993.

190. Bakhtin (note 185), p. 37.

191. Ntozake Shange, *The New York Times*, Op-Ed Section, May 24, 1992.

A New World Every Day
by Dave Hickey

Simone Weil stood in the window of her Paris apartment on the morning of June 14, 1940, and watched the invading German army marching past on the street below. "What a great day for Vietnam," Weil remarked. Those in attendance remember being viscerally shocked by Weil's remark, and perhaps justifiably so, given the catastrophic circumstance in which Parisians found themselves at that moment. Yet, with that single remark, Weil accurately foreshadowed the world in which we live today: the undeniably full, demonstrably round, and increasingly centerless world of postcolonial reality, in which human events, like climatic events, are never isolated nor ever unidirectional.

In this reality, all of those events and actions that constitute our personal, political, and economic lives must be considered irrevocably interconnected and equally subject to the "butterfly effect" that meteorologists evoke to explain how a butterfly flitting from blossom to blossom in a garden in Peking may alter the route of a tornado in Kansas and thus impinge upon the fates of those living in its path. In its political manifestations, the butterfly effect assures us that we live in a full, round, decentered world so intricately constructed and interconnected that a weapon fired in France will echo half a world away, and ultimately come echoing back from some unpredictable direction. Thus, as Weil perceived in the midst of her local catastrophe, imperial aggression in Europe or North America is no more reprehensible and of no more consequence than imperial aggression in Asia, Africa, or Latin America. Nor is the smallest statutory reform in Rhode Island or Rwanda inconsequent to our individual futures.

In this sense, I think, we may take the exhibition "About Place" as emblematic of this new, postcolonial geography, gathering together, as it does, sixteen contemporary artists from across the Western hemisphere whose work is grounded in local experience and/or a sense of place. As one surveys the ebullient admixtures of local sensibility and cosmopolitan practice that pervade this exhibition, in fact, one cannot help but think of Jorge Luis Borges's fable of the map, in which a group of cartographers, at the behest of their emperor and at the apogee of imperial power, construct a map of that empire so explicit and extensive that it exactly covers the territory it describes.

As the empire declines, the giant map is gradually worn away, ultimately surviving only here and there, in scraps and tatters. Borges's fable ends here, with this image of flayed abstraction. But we might extend it, I think, beyond the death of empire and conceive the artists in "About Place" as combining the tatters of that old map with the local realities that it once suppressed, in order to make new artifacts whose power and urgency derive from those local realities—whose mobility and visibility depend upon the shreds and tatters of antique imperial practice that are woven through it, appropriated in each case to new ends. To state the case another way, we might regard these works as demonstrative of a vaguely Hellenistic cultural condition in which the fact that styles are not changing historically (as they have not, in any great degree, since 1970) has enabled the practice of Euro-American art to disperse itself geographically—a cultural condition in which local eccentricity has begun to replace stylistic volatility as the source of that litigious anxiety that we, in this culture, have traditionally taken to signify experience of visual art. Thus, we might see in this exhibition the cultural manifestation of Einstein's theory of relativity, in which the relativity of time and space presents itself to us as the relativity of history and geography—of time slowing down and splintering as space spreads out.

1. Place Dislocated
Having spoken of transportable artworks that are grounded in a local history and imbued with its sense of place, however, we need to address the consequences of exhibiting such works in yet *another* place, within *another* local history. And this returns us to the ancient question of determining the actual "position" of works of art with regard to their many contexts. How, we might ask, does a work of art in a cosmopolitan, historical tradition like our own express its "local history" and its "sense of place" when, within this tradition, the "true subject" of the work is nearly always presumed to be occluded and displaced—when, within this tradition, works of art are presumed to relate to their historical antecedents—to their putative subjects—and to their existing cultural contexts in a dialectical and compensatory manner?

To put it simply, works of art in this Euro-American tradition depend for their very *visibility* upon their ability to violate our local expectations and thus distinguish themselves, within their contexts, as "works of art." Thus, they never stand in a simple one-to-one relationship to these contexts, nor directly express the subjects to which they are addressed. And even if they aspire to do so, we presume that they do not. We presume that works of art aspire to the status of utterances, that they intend to *say* something. In other words, we presume that works of art are secular, historical *images*—that represent some lack or deficiency in the present context. We do not regard them as timeless *icons* whose presence actually fulfills that lack. Moreover, since the status of the image has always been problematic in cosmopolitan Judeo-Christian culture—and even more so since the Reformation—we presume that there is some *reason* for resorting to the image, for preferring it to a simple linguistic statement of the argument, and presume, as well, that this reason is somehow covert.

Thus, we tend to read works of art in a kind of mirror-code, for, unless such works repudiate the past in some degree, unless they reconstitute their subject in some way and dissent to some extent from the visual norms of their contemporary context, they are not *art* by our cultural definition—and simply invisible to us *as* art—however much we might revere them as votive objects. Moreover, most works of art in this tradition not only dissent from their contexts, but *compensate for* deficiencies in these contexts, as well, by making visible that which is lost or absent from that context by imagining that which is desired. Thus, rather than reflecting their contexts, works of art in the West aspire more often than not to *complete* them in a rhetorical sense, to preserve the memory of what is lost, to make present that which is most needfully absent—as a Constable perpetuates the memory of wild landscapes lost in the wake of the enclosure laws—as a Velázquez attributes the power and majesty to King Philip that Spaniards devoutly wished he had—or as a Doris Salcedo perpetuates the present absence of the "disappeared" of Colombia who would otherwise completely vanish.

All of which is simply to say that cosmopolitan Western culture does not produce or reproduce that sort of consensual image about which more ordered and less historical cultures tend to gather, as about a hearth, to celebrate the "presence" of what is represented, its embodiment of truth and antiquity. This culture does produce consensual *texts* that are held in such esteem (laws, constitutions, manifestoes, liturgies, etc.), but the images that we hold in high regard are generally borne aloft on tides of controversy rather than consent—as Leonardo's *Gioconda* and Picasso's *Demoiselles* have maintained themselves within the aura of their problematic. Which is not to say that artists do not *propose* their images as candidates for the status of consensual icons. Certainly all artists who make overtly political and religious imagery aspire to such consent. Certainly Raphael did, as did Mark Rothko and Barnett Newman in their own idiom—and, in fact, many of Rothko's images present themselves almost literally as hearths around which the culture might commune. Finally, however, we must read Rothko's images, and Newman's as well, and even Raphael's, as compensatory *proposals* for consensual iconography within a litigious, cosmopolitan discourse—as arguments *for* a consensual iconography that is demonstrably absent from the culture—and not as consensual icons themselves. We may see the twilight of this totalizing aspiration, I think, considerably attenuated and aware of its contingency, in Brice Marden's paintings in this exhibition, which preserve for us less the urgency of Rothko's aspiration than the loveliness and generosity of the sentiment.

Having said that Western culture does not produce consensual images, however, we must remember that many images designed to function argumentatively in one context have been routinely *adopted* as consensual icons in another context within the cosmopolis—which is simply to say that images and objects travel more easily than the arguments that inform them. Thus, an argumentative image developed in seventeenth-century Spain as a part of the great theological quarrel surrounding the Reformation and the Counter Reformation, will be transformed into a full, mystical, consensual icon when transported to Latin America and isolated from the cosmopolitan iconography of that quarrel.

This sensitivity of Western images to their contexts, I would suggest, constitutes the unabating difficulty that confronts any artist who addresses regional concerns within a widely dispersed practice. No one doubts, for instance, that the fierce adversarial position maintained by Anselm Kiefer's paintings with regard to postwar German culture dissolves into an aura of cozy familiarity on the east side of Manhattan—nor do they doubt that the tough dissent from Southern California values that is manifest in the sculpture of Edward Kienholz all but disappears into the brickwork in Berlin. Yet Kiefers continue to wing their way west as Kienholz's work flies east.

Nor does anyone doubt that the paintings of Frederic Remington were designed to be everything that New York City, at the turn of this century, was not and longed to be, since New York, at this time, was neither France nor Arizona. As a consequence,

in the mirror language of Western painting, Remington's Frenchified genre paintings of the American West speak volumes about the visual proclivities of haute bourgeois culture in New York at the beginning of this century. We see in Remington's paintings the shadow of belle-époque desire: the longing for a more robust imagery rendered in a more refined *peinture*, the need for images of a simpler, less class-ridden culture, portrayed in a trendier, more class-conscious style.

Still, we learn very little about French painting, or about Arizona landscape, from Remington's pictures beyond the fact that the citizens of Arizona and other Western states, by adopting Remington's pastiche as an authentic, empowering vision, transformed his colonizing images into iconic cultural presences—as the citizens of Santa Fe and Taos would bestow the mantle of iconicity upon the images of colonizing modernists like Marsden Hartley and Georgia O'Keeffe—as the culture of Latin America would embrace the colonizing rhetoric of the Spanish Baroque. All of which is to say that, in the practice of Euro-American art, it is exactly this aspiration to consensual iconicity that distinguishes provincial from cosmopolitan practice—however one wishes to value these distinct endeavors. Further, I would suggest that the willingness of the artists in this exhibition to address local realities *within* a cosmopolitan practice is exactly what distinguishes their work from the "regionalisms" of the past.

In any case, we may safely assume, I think, that the visual content of any Euro-American art that is self-consciously about "place," is likely to be routinely, and often radically, displaced from the locale that constitutes its true subject. We may assume, for instance, that an Impressionist painting tells us less about the look of suburban France, than it does about the urban culture that it displaces; and in this mirror-language, we may read the Japanese-Disney winterscapes into which Larry Johnson has set his narratives of gay Hollywood as displacements of desire that relate to Los Angeles in much the same way that Remington's Western landscapes relate to belle-époque New York—only more self-consciously. And we may find the imperial double-vision that allowed Remington to colonize Arizona subtly parodied in Jeff Wall's photoscapes in which quotidian North America is shrewdly—and almost subliminally—tricked up in the pictorial conventions of high European painting.

Thus, the primary portrayals of "natural places" in this exhibition—those of Rodney Graham and Vija Celmins—are radically dislocated from the nature they represent by the conventions and mechanics of photography, so the images themselves, cropped, tipped, or inverted, are torn free from their "natural setting" and located in the eye of the beholder, so we know that the real "place" under scrutiny is, in fact, the cultural position from which we purport to view nature. Graham's and Celmins's images, then, suppress the vertical/horizontal language of landscape representation in order to defamiliarize and dislocate our access to nature.

In so doing, Graham and Celmins break the connection that ties our bodily orientation to the horizontal and the vertical and to the political implications of the horizontal and the vertical in Western images. This connection, of course, equates bodily equilibrium with centrality and virtue (the sign of the cross) and allows

Fig. 37.
Terry Allen (American, born 1943)
APARTE (rat talk at the Sonic), 1988
Mixed media
48⅜ x 48⅜ x 9 inches
(122.9 x 122.9 x 22.9 cm)
Collection of Clyde and Karen
Beswick, Los Angeles

us to presume, as Barbara Steinman ironically proclaims, that
"the center of the world is exactly where you stand." This assump-
tion, of course, allows us to regard any position other than our
own (at the "center of the world") as somehow "off the vertical"—
as not "upright" and somehow less than virtuous, as slightly ques-
tionable and imperfect—as marginal by definition. We may see the
political aspects of Celmins's and Graham's subversion of pictorial
equilibrium theatricalized in a series of images by Terry Allen called
Youth in Asia. In this series, Allen violates our expectations of a congruent vertical and horizontal pictorial environment in hopes of por-
traying the "global" nature of the American experience of Vietnam.
To do this, he displaces images at angles off the vertical (sometimes
tilted, sometimes sideways, sometimes inverted) to designate the
source of the image on the round world and to infer its distance
from (and dissonance within) the controlling consciousness of the
beholder, which is the "home" of the image itself.

  Still, the question remains: how can a work of art installed
in one place speak to us through its displaced subject-matter about
its absent subject? In what sense, in other words, is a painting by
Tiepolo that hangs on a wall in Rome and portrays Anthony and
Cleopatra in Egypt, still a Venetian picture? Certainly, it comments
indirectly on Venetian mercantile concerns. And, just as certainly,
Tiepolo's practice is grounded in the tradition of Venetian painting.
And, yes, the "Egyptian" sky glows as the sky does in Venice and
the light dances in that Venetian way—and even the *peinture* seems
on the verge of crumbling as the walls of Venice have always
seemed about to do. But this is no real answer unless we take Terry
Allen's inference and locate the work of art, as a cultural signifier,
in the bodily memory of its beholders. We must assume, I think,
that we, as beholders, are creatures of our times and that the conditions of a full and interdependent global culture may be inscribed
in our bodily memories in a language of absences and imaginary
compensations—and assume, finally, that any work of art that
seems to be telling us exactly what we want to hear, is not speaking
in its true voice.

2. Time Dehistoricized

When considering "About Place" as an exhibition, I think it helps
to remember that most exhibitions that have taken "places" as their
subject propose to isolate historical origins and demonstrate historical influences. They suggest the larger historical consequences
of specific regional practices (Sienese painting, German Minimalism, etc.), or they seek to demonstrate the regional consequences of various cosmopolitan practices (the impact of Greek
sculptural practice on its Alexandrian descendants, etc.). In either
case, a unidirectional narrative is implied and some shift of power
is presumed to take place between the presumed center and the
presumed periphery. As a consequence, the works in such exhibitions tend to be considered according to their power to evoke,
manifest, or demonstrate historical forces within a unidirectional
temporal flux.

  In other words, these exhibitions take "time" as their subject, so that we might think differently about "place." "About Place,"
however, takes "place" as its subject, and, by dislocating and diffus-
ing it, allows us to think differently about "time." More specifically,
this exhibition takes "geography" as its subject so that we may think
differently about "history." Rather than demonstrating the source or
influence of some canonical practice, this exhibition presents us with
disparate manifestations of various post-Minimal strategies that dif-
fer from one another according to their geopolitical occasion and
local political agendas. As a consequence, this exhibition proposes
art history as a skein of little, local "art histories," each of which is
intertwined with numerous other local histories—personal, political,
and climatic—all of which intersect in the occasion of the work.
Therefore, within this context, even the paintings of Brice Marden,
which represent the most "canonical" practice in the exhibition,
function here as "regional art," as images deeply imbricated in their
own local history—that of New York painting.

  The simplest way to characterize this conceptual inversion from *time* as *the container of places* to *place* as *the container
of times*—is to consider it as analogous to the transformation

that Michel Foucault proposes in the *Archeology of Knowledge*, when he suggests that we reconstitute the allegorical "history of thought" as a static "field of discourse" and transform its narrative of linguistic events into a constellation of distinct "statements," each occupying its own discrete micro-location. In the case of "About Place," I think, we must reconceive the location of culture (which we usually think of as a static locale) as a vortex of multiple, multidirectional, local micro-narratives rather in the way that the cultural location of Jac Leirner's accumulations may be defined as the point where the individual micro-history of each purloined object intersects.

The primary virtue of this inversion, I think, is that it allows us to see so-called "dominant historical styles" for what they are: fictional constructions brought into being by suppressing the local eccentricities that pervade their every material instance. The effect of this transformation is to propose "place" as the predicate of "time"—*time is place*—rather than "time" as the predicate of "place"—*place is time*—which, I hasten to note, is more easily said than done—and more easily done than perceived, since all the spatio-temporal metaphors of Western civilization, from Moses to Marx, conspire against it. This degree of difficulty, however, demonstrates the urgency of the task, since our reflexive shunting of works of art out of local experience into theory-driven, quasihistorical, stylistic hyperspace is probably the single greatest contributor to the trivialization of art at the present moment.

Still, the habit of thinking of time as the container of places is deeply ingrained. For Westerners in the late twentieth century, it would seem, places are contingent, while time is presumed to be their monolithic and unidirectional container. And although we may wish to reconstitute the idea of place as a vortex of specified local histories, that condition, in Western civilization, remains reserved for *central* places, for cultural destinations where time may be presumed to reside. Thus, history may be presumed to *accumulate* in Athens or Rome, in London, Paris, or New York, while it *flows through* and subjugates every place else.

The entire metaphorical construction of our civilization, in fact, drives us to consider time as a litany of places. Lines from old songs ("Life is like a mountain railway"), the images of Huck and Jim on their raft, of Ulysses tied to his mast, of Gary Cooper riding off into the sunset, all arise to remind us of this linear imperative. We are the children of motion, it would seem, obsessed with departures times and ETAs. So, time *is* a place for us, and physical places exist to mark its temporal occasions. Thus, we think of our lives as journeys and construct our meta-narratives in terms of location and domain, imagining the past and projecting the future onto the geographer's palimpsest, making time into a map where distance is measured in minutes and location determined by time displaced from its equatorial norm.

Upon this map, which is, of course, Borges's map, history is a dance of arrows and traverses—of expanding and receding stains of territorial hegemony that spread out from points of originary power and intersect at points of marginal consequence, erupting there into violence and entropy. And even though we *know* that history is not one map but many overlaid, we tend to stratify these histories at their points of overlap and intersection. We assume that the slow dance of geological time, the turbulent progress of wind and weather, the rough, quick history of local politics and the stately progress of culture and geopolitics pass under and above one another in the place where we stand amidst the narrative of our own lives. And it is this construct of stratified histories that Ann Hamilton seeks to collapse in her installations which, taken en masse, constitute a series of vertical cuts down through these strata in order to collapse the rhetorics of human "nature" and agri "culture," of personal histories and historical personalities into singular, complex local occasions.

Still, we continue to speak of history as we always have, as a litany of positioned places: of origins, capitals, intersections, turning points and destinations: Athens, Rome, Carthage, Agincourt, Waterloo, Worms, Trent, Soweto, Bethlehem, Jerusalem, Eden; and this leaves us with the linguistic illusion, if not the belief, that history is going some *place*—that it arrives at the "margins" in the same condition that it departs from the "center" that our cultural narrative, in its singular one-way motion, inevitably approaches some metaphysical location. Poets may tell us otherwise, as Shelley does, as Conrad does in "Heart of Darkness," but we continue to behave as if this were true, as if we were "on our way"—even though we know that the Earth is a globe, that every place is in the same place upon it, that a journey in any direction will end where it began, that temporal sequences depart uniformly from every point and arrive from every direction.

Thus, as twentieth-century humans, we are comfortable with Einstein's reminder that time and space are relative and that energy and matter coextend. The relativity of history and geography, however, is harder for us to grasp. We have assumed for so long that we are all one in our historical moment that the idea of our all being different in our geographical occasion seems vaguely apocalyptic. Yet it doesn't take a genius to perceive that even the simple micro-narrative of art history has its streams and cross currents—that European art history, for instance, breaks into tributaries as it flows west into the Americas—so that the "European art history" that flows through Latin America suppresses the Reformation, elides the Enlightenment and jumps almost directly from the tortured flesh of Ribera to the tortured flesh of Delacroix—that the art history that dominates the Northern tier of the United States and Canada occludes both the Catholic Renaissance and the hedonism of Mediterranean antiquity, sustaining itself in the medieval rhetoric of the grotesque body and the iconoclasm of Anglo-German Protestantism—while, in the Southern tier of the United States, the Catholic iconophilia of Latin America is hedonized and the Protestant conceptualism of Northern America is radically secularized. Add into this, the dispersion of indigenous and postcolonial iconographies, the counter-flow of Oriental influences from the East and the dissemination of post-World War II influences out of New York and Los Angeles, and assume further that all styles are local, that nothing arrives in the condition it departs and you will understand the extent to which geography has subsumed history as the first condition of cultural urbanity in the late twentieth century, and understand, as well, the mysterious anxiety that must of necessity pervade its fluidity and interdependence.

Plates

Plates

Vija Celmins Born in Riga, Latvia, lives in New York

Plate 1.
Vija Celmins
Night Sky #2, 1991
Oil on canvas mounted on aluminum
Courtesy McKee Gallery, New York
Cat. no. 2

Plate 2.
Vija Celmins
Desert Surface #1, 1991
Oil on wood panel
Collection of Harry W. and Mary Margaret Anderson
Cat. no. 1

Plate 3.
Vija Celmins
Web, 1992
Oil on canvas
Collection of the artist, courtesy McKee Gallery, New York
Cat. no. 4

Eugenio Dittborn Born and lives in Santiago, Chile

Plate 4.
Eugenio Dittborn
Airmail Painting No. 95:
The 13th History of the Human Face
(The Portals of H.), 1991
Courtesy Airmail Paintings Inc.
Cat. no. 6

Plate 5.
Airmail Painting No. 95 (detail)

Plate 6.
Eugenio Dittborn
Photograph of source materials
for *Airmail Painting No. 113:
On La Grande Jatte, Final Version
of a Sunday*, 1994–95

The picture shows two superimposed open books. The
largest of the two is a publication that includes newspapers from the period of the Guerra del Pacífico (War
of the Pacific), reprinted on the occasion of that war's
centennial. The smaller book is a publication by The
Art Institute of Chicago dedicated to the painting
A Sunday on La Grande Jatte—1884 by Georges
Seurat. Both books were used by Eugenio Dittborn in
the production of Airmail Painting No. 113.

—Eugenio Dittborn

Plate 7. (Right)
Santiago de Chile, corner of Calle
Bandera and Paseo Ahumada,
July 1993.

October: Production Diary of Airmail Painting No. 113

Eugenio Dittborn

Translated by Paul Beuchat   Santiago de Chile

October 2, 1994: For three weeks now, I have been searching in vain for a title to give my version of Seurat's work.

October 8, 1994: "Sunday Afternoon on the Island of La Grande Jatte" is the title of the painting by Seurat that appears in the Art Institute's publication. Two secretly analogous things fascinate me in that title: Sunday afternoon (the endless time of an empty desert) and the possibility of imagining the figures in Seurat's painting as the inhabitants of an island (life saving board for shipwrecked survivors and place of confinement).

October 9, 1994: In the same Art Institute publication I noticed in a reproduction of Seurat's painting, a widespread use of costumes of all kinds: from figures in undershirts to couples dressed up to go to the opera, soldiers, one figure playing a wind instrument, suntanned little girls. All these figures appear to be acting out a Sunday.

On the other hand, none of the bodies painted by Seurat seem to inhabit common ground; instead, they occupy multiple fragments that could be the consequence of an explosion (notice the woman on the left with a fishing rod in her right hand. Isn't she a Sunday fisherman, just like a Sunday painter?)

October 14, 1994: The particles or dots in the work painted by Seurat appear to be the consequence of some mechanism such as Parkinson's disease: an uncontrollable tic, touching and marking the entire surface of the canvas. Each dot or particle was painted by Seurat in an instant of production different from that of every other dot: a multiplicity beyond calculation of production micro-times. In photography, on the contrary, the entire surface is produced instantaneously.

October 22, 1994: Today, through Madeleine Grynsztejn, I have found out that the official title of the work by Seurat, recently declared as the definitive one, is "A Sunday on La Grande Jatte—1884." Almost immediately, I came up with the title for my version of Seurat's work: "On La Grande Jatte, Final Version of a Sunday."

October 31, 1994: Today, I have finally found a power line through which to begin my version of Seurat's painting: putting fragments of it in close contact with photographs of the scenarios of the war between Chile and an alliance between Peru and Bolivia in 1879, five years before Seurat began working on "A Sunday on La Grande Jatte."

The scenario of the war of "La Guerra del Pacífico" (The War of the Pacific), which is how it is known, was the desert north of Chile and the ocean on that same latitude. Chile won the war, and usurped vast territories belonging to Peru and Bolivia. My purpose is to render visible the incalculable distance between the painted Grande Jatte in Paris, capital of the XIX Century—as Walter Benjamin put it—and the photographed scenarios of a war at the end of the world. Paradoxically, that distance can only be rendered visible by putting closer—until they crash—"A Sunday on La Grande Jatte" and the Chilean desert, separated by an abyss. For that contact to be possible and

Leonardo Drew Born in Tallahassee, Florida, lives in New York

Leonardo Drew Born in Tallahassee, Florida, lives in New York

Plate 8.
Leonardo Drew
Number 43, 1994
Wood, rust, fabric, string, and mixed media
Courtesy of the artist and Tim Nye, New York
Cat. no. 8

Plate 9.
Number 43 (detail)

Felix Go

...nzalez-Torres Born in Guáimaro, Cuba, lives in New York

Plate 10.
Felix Gonzalez-Torres
Untitled (Arena), 1993
Sixty lightbulbs, extension cord, porcelain
light sockets, and dimmer switch
Installation view: Galerie Jennifer Flay, Paris,
"Travels #2," Oct. 30–Dec. 1, 1993
Private Collection, Germany

Plate 11.
Felix Gonzalez-Torres
Untitled (Summer), 1993
Forty-two lightbulbs, extension cord,
and porcelain light sockets
Courtesy Andrea Rosen Gallery,
New York

Plate 12.
Felix Gonzalez-Torres
Untitled (Strange Bird), 1993
Billboard
Location: Crenshaw Boulevard and 48th Street,
Los Angeles
Installed as part of
The Museum of Contemporary Art, Los Angeles,
"Traveling," Apr. 24–June 19, 1994

Plate 13.
Felix Gonzalez-Torres
Untitled, 1991–93, and *Untitled (Arena)*, 1993
Two billboards; sixty lightbulbs, extension cord,
porcelain light sockets, and dimmer switch
Private Collection, Germany

Rodney Graham Born in Matsqui, British Columbia, Canada, lives in Vancouver

Plate 14.
Rodney Graham
Millenial Project for an Urban Plaza (with Cappuccino Bar), 1992
Architectural model with the collaboration of Robert Kleyn
Plexiglas, brass, and painted iron base
Fonds Régional d'Art Contemporain du Centre, Orléans, France
Cat. no. 11

Plate 15.
Rodney Graham, *Stanley Park, Cedar #4*, 1993
C–print from black-and-white negative
Courtesy Galerie Nelson, Paris
Cat. no. 14

Plate 16.
Rodney Graham, *Stanley Park, Cedar #5,* 1993
C–print from black-and-white negative
Fonds Régional d'Art Contemporain Bretagne, France
Cat. no. 15

Ann Hamilton Born in Lima, Ohio, lives in Columbus

Plate 17.
Ann Hamilton
lineament, 1994
Installation view: Ruth Bloom Gallery,
Santa Monica, California,
June 4–July 17, 1994
Courtesy Sean Kelly, New York

Plate 18.
lineament (detail)

Plate 19.
Ann Hamilton
aleph, 1992
Installation view: MIT List Visual Arts
Center, Cambridge, Massachussetts,
Oct. 9–Nov. 22, 1992
Courtesy Sean Kelly, New York

Larry Johnson Born in Long Beach, California, lives in Los Angeles

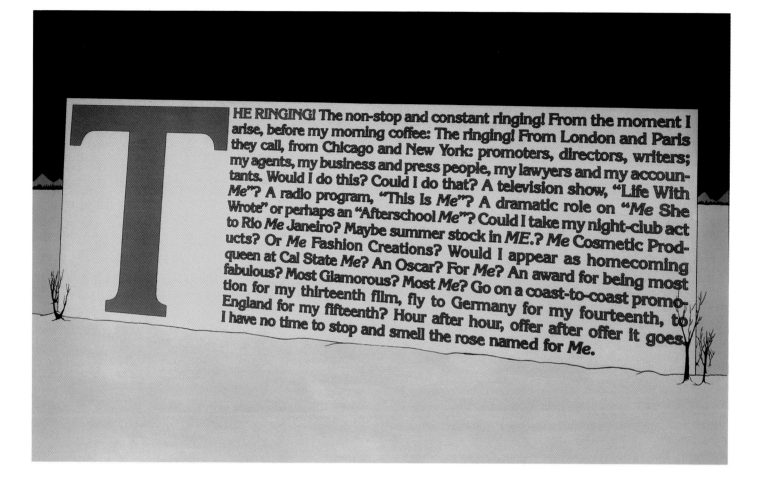

Plate 21.
Larry Johnson
Untitled (Standing Still & Walking in Los Angeles), 1994
Ektacolor photograph
Edition 1/3
The Museum of Contemporary Art, Los Angeles,
purchased with funds provided by James and Linda Burrows
Cat. no. 24

Plate 22.
Larry Johnson
Untitled (Negative H), 1993
Ektacolor photograph (unique)
Courtesy Margo Leavin Gallery, Los Angeles
Cat. no. 22

Guillermo Kuitca Born and lives in Buenos Aires, Argentina

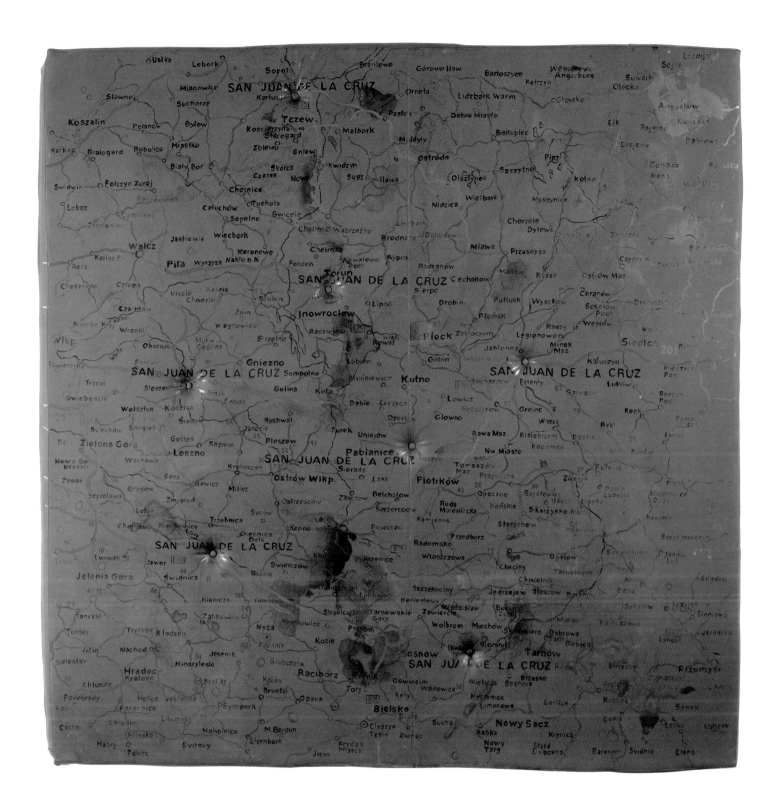

Plate 23.
Guillermo Kuitca
San Juan de la Cruz, 1992
Mixed media on mattress
Courtesy Sperone Westwater, New York
Cat. no. 27

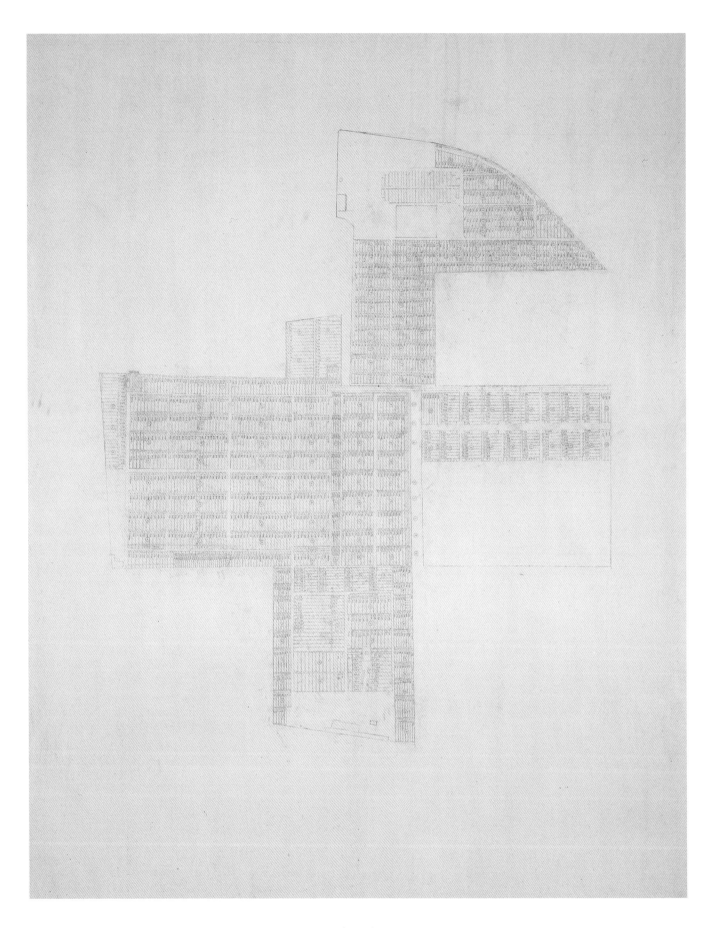

Plate 24.
Guillermo Kuitca
The Tablada Suite I, 1991
Graphite and acrylic on canvas
Courtesy Sperone Westwater, New York
Cat. no. 26

Plate 25.
Guillermo Kuitca
Planta con fondo blanco [Plan with White Background], 1989
Acrylic on canvas
Courtesy Sperone Westwater, New York
Cat. no. 25

Jac Leirner Born and lives in São Paulo, Brazil

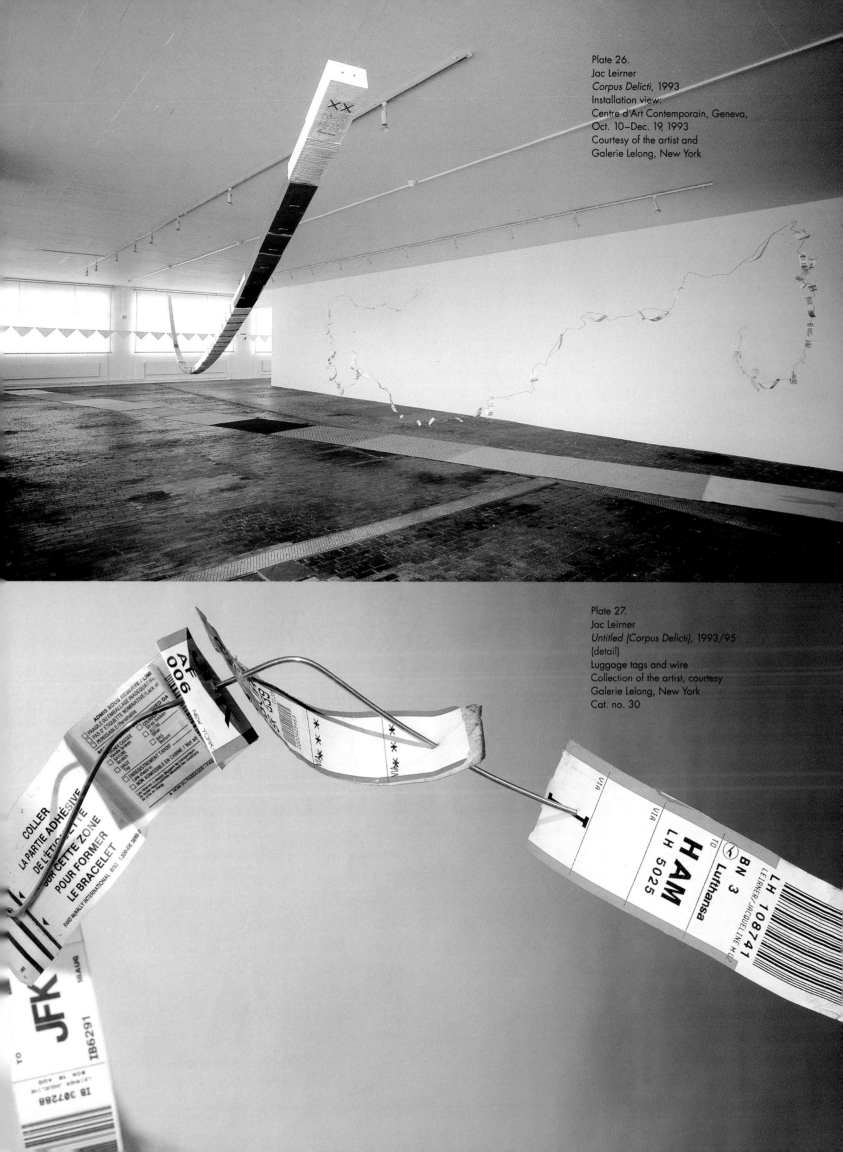

Plate 26.
Jac Leirner
Corpus Delicti, 1993
Installation view:
Centre d'Art Contemporain, Geneva,
Oct. 10–Dec. 19, 1993
Courtesy of the artist and
Galerie Lelong, New York

Plate 27.
Jac Leirner
Untitled {Corpus Delicti}, 1993/95
(detail)
Luggage tags and wire
Collection of the artist, courtesy
Galerie Lelong, New York
Cat. no. 30

Plate 28.
Jac Leirner
*Os Cem (roda) [The One Hundreds
(wheel)]*, 1986
Banknotes and steel
2¾ x 31½ inches
(7 x 80 cm) diameter
Collection of Marcantonio Vilaça,
São Paulo

Plate 29.
Jac Leirner
Os Cem [The One Hundreds], 1986
Banknotes and polyurethane cord
Two parts, each 2¾ x 6¼ x 118⅛
inches (7 x 15 x 300 cm)
Collection of André L'Huillier, Geneva

Plates 30 and 31.
Jac Leirner
Untitled (Corpus Delicti), 1993
Forks, knives, and spoons from
various airlines, and polyurethane cord
The Bohen Foundation
Cat. no. 29

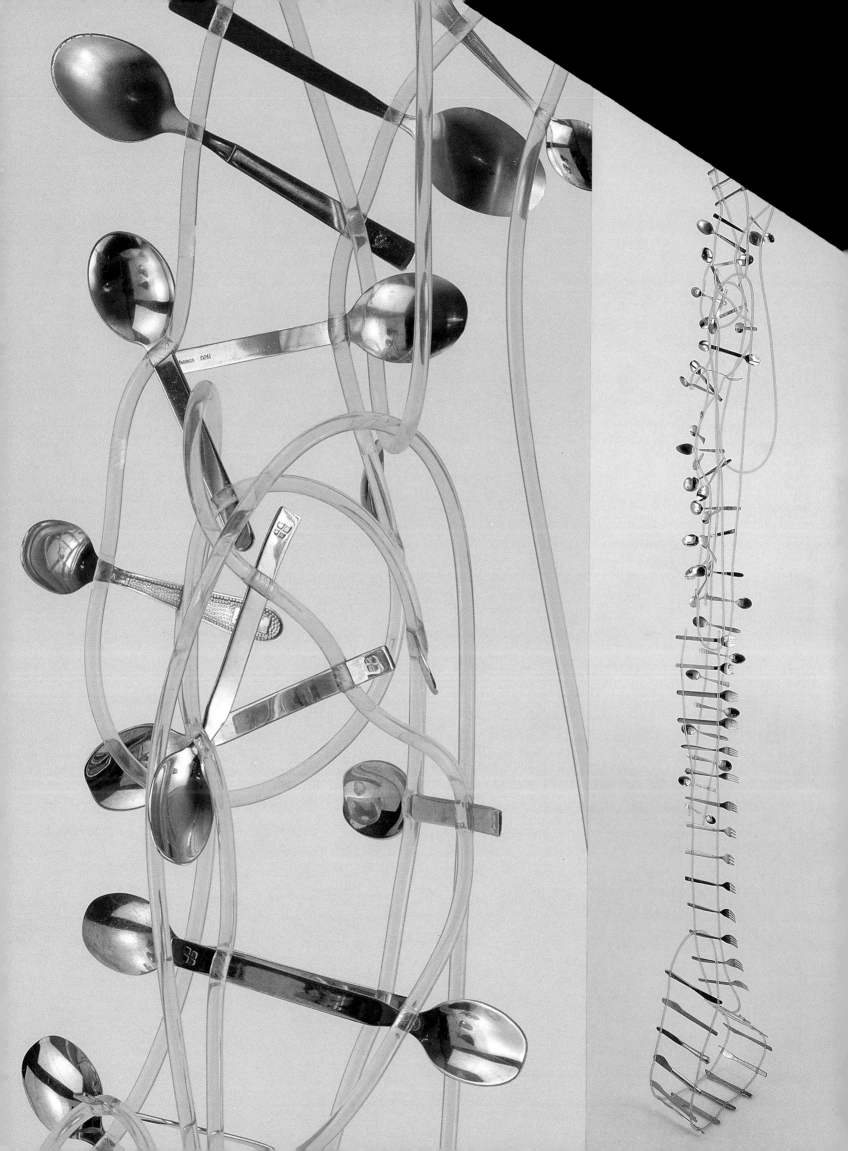

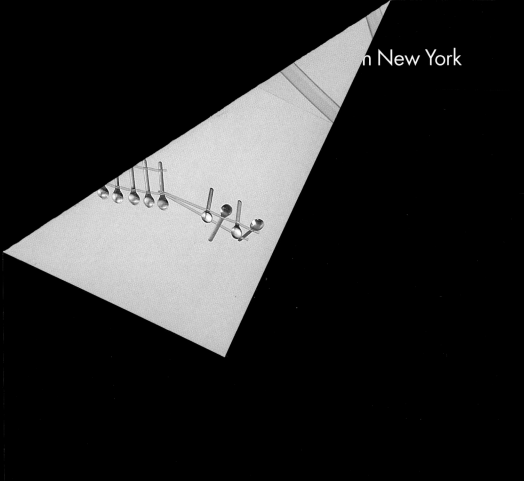

n New York

Plate 32.
Brice Marden
The Sisters, 1991–93
Oil on linen
Private Collection, San Francisco
Cat. no. 32

Plate 33. (Left)
Brice Marden
February in Hydra, 1991–94
Oil on linen
135 x 83 inches (342.9 x 210.8 cm)
Courtesy Matthew Marks Gallery,
New York

Plate 34.
Brice Marden
Corpus, 1992–94
Oil on linen
Froelich Collection, Stuttgart
Cat. no. 33

Kerry James Marshall Born in Birmingham, Alabama, lives in Chicago

Plate 35.
Kerry James Marshall
Many Mansions, 1994
Acrylic and collage on canvas
Courtesy of the artist and Koplin Gallery, Santa Monica
Cat. no. 39

Plate 36.
Kerry James Marshall
C.H.I.A., 1994
Acrylic and collage on canvas
Courtesy of the artist and Koplin Gallery, Santa Monica
Cat. no. 38

102

Plate 37.
Kerry James Marshall
Better Homes Better Gardens, 1994
Acrylic and collage on canvas
Courtesy of the artist and Jack Shainman Gallery, New York
Cat. no. 37

Doris Salcedo Born and lives in Bogotá, Colombia

Plate 38.
Doris Salcedo
Atrabiliarios [Defiant], 1992
Wall installation with plywood, shoes,
animal fiber, and surgical thread
Installation view: Institute of
Contemporary Art, Boston,
Jan. 22–Mar. 22, 1992
Courtesy Brooke Alexander, New York

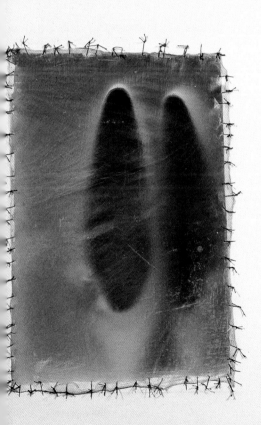
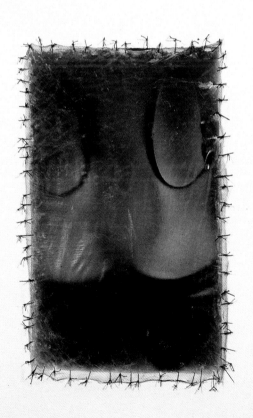
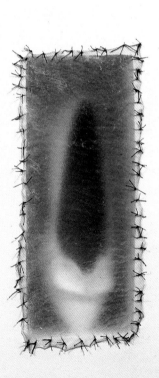

Plate 39.
Atrabiliarios [Defiant] (detail)

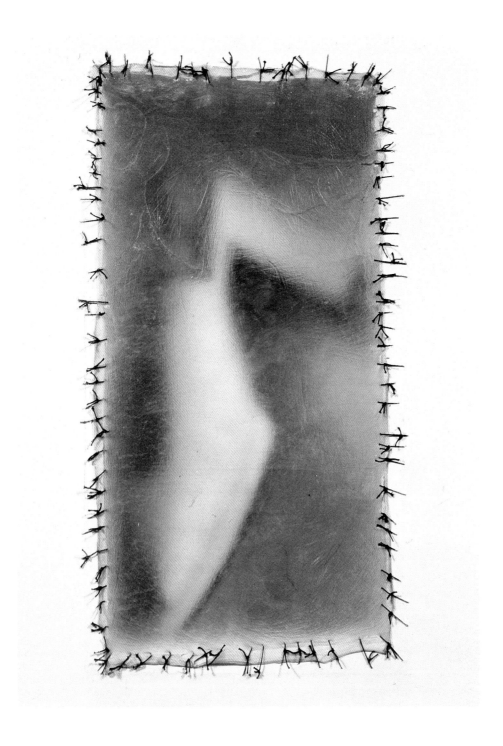

Plate 40.
Doris Salcedo
Atrabiliarios [Defiant] (detail)

Plate 41.
Doris Salcedo
Atrabiliarios [Defiant], 1993
Nazareno wood, six shoes, animal fiber, and surgical thread
78¾ x 39½ x 3⅝ inches (200 x 100 x 8 cm)
Courtesy Brooke Alexander, New York

Anna Deavere Smith Born in Baltimore, Maryland, lives in San Francisco

Plate 42.
Anna Deavere Smith
as the Reverend Al Sharpton
*Fires in the Mirror: Crown Heights,
Brooklyn and Other Identities*, 1992

Plate 43.
Anna Deavere Smith
as Letty Cottin Pogrebin
*Fires in the Mirror: Crown Heights,
Brooklyn and Other Identities*, 1992

Plate 44.
Anna Deavere Smith
as Angela King, aunt of Rodney King
Twilight: Los Angeles, 1992
Mark Taper Forum, Los Angeles,
June 13–July 18, 1993

Plate 45.
Anna Deavere Smith
as Rueven Ostrov, Lubavitscher youth,
member of Project CURE
*Fires in the Mirror: Crown Heights,
Brooklyn and Other Identities, 1992*

Plate 46.
Anna Deavere Smith
as Anonymous Young Man #2
*Fires in the Mirror: Crown Heights,
Brooklyn and Other Identities*, 1992

Plate 47.
Anna Deavere Smith
as Reginald Denny
Twilight: Los Angeles, 1992
Mark Taper Forum, Los Angeles,
June 13–July 18, 1993

Barbara Steinman Born and lives in Montreal, Quebec, Canada

Plate 48 and inset. (Previous page)
Barbara Steinman
Objects and Instruments, 1992
Map on rose window,
24 inscribed lenses in brass tripods
Installation view:
Chapelle de l'Hôtel-Dieu, Troyes, France,
June 26–Sept. 12, 1992
Courtesy of the artist and Olga Korper
Gallery, Toronto
Cat. no. 45

Plates 49 and 50.
Barbara Steinman
L'Ecoute [Gesture], 1992
Two cibachrome pearl photographs
Edition 1/5
Collection of Alison and Alan
Schwartz
Cat. no. 44

Jeff Wall Born and lives in Vancouver, British Columbia, Canada

Plate 51.
Jeff Wall
Fight on the Sidewalk, 1994
Cibachrome transparency, fluorescent light, and display case
Collection of Jordi Soley, Barcelona
Cat. no. 48

Andrea Zittel Born in Escondido, California, lives in Brooklyn

Introducing

Co-Authorship of A-Z products

A-Z believes that there are two authors for every product we make...
one author is A-Z, and the other is you!

ADMINISTRATIVE SERVICES
A-Z
ZITTEL

Photos courtesy of Andrea Rosen Gallery, New York
Photography by Peter Muscato
Design by Jean Garrett

Please send documentation of products you have redesigned to:
A-Z Administrative Services, 150 Wythe Avenue, Brooklyn, NY 11211

You can author any product by using it in your own way

Colors and accessories are traditional tactics of authorship

Once you use a product, you are an expert

You can create guidelines of taste and utility to help manage the responsibility of authorship

Design does not stop with manufacture

Plate 54.
Andrea Zittel
Artist's proposal for catalogue spread, created for the exhibition
"About Place: Recent Art of the Americas," 1994
Courtesy of the artist and Andrea Rosen Gallery, New York

Plates 55–59.
Andrea Zittel
A to Z Comfort Units I and II, 1994
Steel, birch plywood, velvet, Plexiglas,
foam mattress, and objects
Courtesy of the artist, Andrea Rosen Gallery, New York,
and Anthony d'Offay Gallery, London

Catalogue of the Exhibition

Height precedes width precedes depth; dimensions are given in inches and centimeters unless otherwise specified.

Vija Celmins

1. *Desert Surface #1,* 1991
Oil on wood panel
18⅛ x 21⅝ inches (46 x 55 cm)
Collection of Harry W. and
Mary Margaret Anderson
Plate 2

2. *Night Sky #2,* 1991
Oil on canvas mounted on aluminum
18 x 21½ inches (45.7 x 54.6 cm)
Courtesy McKee Gallery, New York
Plate 1

3. *Desert Surface #2,* 1992
Oil on canvas
19½ x 22½ inches (49.5 x 57 cm)
Collection of the artist, courtesy
McKee Gallery, New York

4. *Web,* 1992
Oil on canvas
18¾ x 22¼ inches (47.6 x 56.5 cm)
Collection of the artist, courtesy
McKee Gallery, New York
Plate 3

5. *Night Sky #7,* 1995
Oil on canvas
38 x 47 inches (96.5 x 119.4 cm)
Courtesy McKee Gallery, New York

Eugenio Dittborn

6. *Airmail Painting No. 95: The 13th History of the Human Face (The Portals of H.),* 1991
Paint, stitching, and photosilkscreen on 6 sections of nonwoven fabric
Dimensions vary with installation (from 137¾ x 330¹¹⁄₁₆ inches [350 x 840 cm] to 137¾ x 220½ inches [350 x 560 cm])
Courtesy Airmail Paintings Inc.
Plates 4 and 5; figure 12

7. *Airmail Painting No. 113: On la Grande Jatte, Final Version of a Sunday,* 1994–95
Paint, stitching, and photosilkscreen on 5 sections of cotton fabric (Crea)
137¾ x 165⅜ inches (350 x 420 cm)
Courtesy Airmail Paintings Inc.

Leonardo Drew

8. *Number 43,* 1994
Wood, rust, fabric, string, and mixed media
137½ x 287½ x 4 inches (349.3 x 730.3 x 10.2 cm)
Courtesy of the artist and Tim Nye, New York
Plates 8 and 9

Felix Gonzalez-Torres

9. *Untitled (America),* 1993
From one to twelve light strings, each consisting of 42 lightbulbs, extension cord, rubber light sockets, and dimmer switch
Dimensions vary with installation
Courtesy of the artist and Andrea Rosen Gallery, New York

Rodney Graham

10. *Reading Machine for Lenz,* 1983/93
Printed paper, glass, Plexiglas, stainless steel, and wood
21¾ x 23½ x 7¾ inches at base (55.2 x 59.7 x 19.7 cm)
Edition 1/3
Private Collection, London
Figure 7

11. *Millenial Project for an Urban Plaza (with Cappuccino Bar),* 1992
Architectural model with the collaboration of Robert Kleyn
Plexiglas, brass, and painted iron base
Maquette: 27¾ x 26 x 17⅓ inches (70.5 x 66.2 x 44.2 cm)
Fonds Régional d'Art Contemporain du Centre, Orléans, France
Plate 14

12. *Stanley Park, Cedar #2,* 1993
C–print from black-and-white negative
105 x 72 inches (267 x 183 cm)
Musée Départemental de Rochechouart, France

13. *Stanley Park, Cedar #3,* 1993
C–print from black-and-white negative
105 x 72 inches (267 x 183 cm)
Courtesy Galerie Nelson, Paris

14. *Stanley Park, Cedar #4,* 1993
C–print from black-and-white negative
105 x 72 inches (267 x 183 cm)
Courtesy Galerie Nelson, Paris
Plate 15

15. *Stanley Park, Cedar #5,* 1993
C–print from black-and-white negative
105 x 72 inches (267 x 183 cm)
Fonds Régional d'Art Contemporain Bretagne, France
Plate 16

16. *Stanley Park, Cedar #6,* 1993
C–print from black-and-white negative
105 x 72 inches (267 x 183 cm)
Courtesy Galerie Nelson, Paris

17. *Stanley Park, Cedar #7,* 1993
C–print from black-and-white negative
105 x 72 inches (267 x 183 cm)
National Gallery of Canada, Ottawa

Ann Hamilton

18. *volumen,* 1995
Site-specific installation in the Loggia, Gallery 264, of The Daniel F. and Ada L. Rice Building at The Art Institute of Chicago
Mechanical ceiling track with rotating hanging curtain
Overall dimensions 270 x 724 x 102 inches (685.8 x 1839 x 259.1 cm)
Courtesy Sean Kelly, New York

Larry Johnson

19. *Untitled (ABC),* 1990
Ektacolor photograph
60 x 49 inches framed
(152.5 x 124.5 cm)
Edition 2/3
Courtesy Margo Leavin Gallery,
Los Angeles

20. *Untitled (Winter Me),* 1990
Ektacolor photograph (unique)
61 x 86¹/₂ inches framed
(155 x 220 cm)
Collection of Richard Prince
Plate 20

21. *Untitled (Classically Tragic
Story),* 1991
Ektacolor photograph
49 x 61 inches framed
(124.5 x 155 cm)
Edition 3/3
Courtesy Margo Leavin Gallery,
Los Angeles

22. *Untitled (Negative H),* 1993
Ektacolor photograph (unique)
56¹/₂ x 79 inches framed
(143.5 x 200.6 cm)
Courtesy Margo Leavin Gallery,
Los Angeles
Plate 22

23. *Untitled (Admit Nothing),* 1994
Ektacolor photograph
45³/₄ x 58⁷/₈ inches framed
(116.2 x 149.5 cm)
Edition 1/3
Courtesy Margo Leavin Gallery,
Los Angeles
Figure 33

24. *Untitled (Standing Still & Walking
in Los Angeles),* 1994
Ektacolor photograph
45⁷/₈ x 87¹/₄ inches framed
(116.5 x 221.6 cm)
Edition 1/3
The Museum of Contemporary Art,
Los Angeles, purchased with funds
provided by James and Linda Burrows
Plate 21

Guillermo Kuitca

25. *Planta con fondo blanco [Plan
with White Background],* 1989
Acrylic on canvas
77¹/₂ x 54¹/₂ inches
(196.9 x 138.4 cm)
Courtesy Sperone Westwater,
New York
Plate 25

26. *The Tablada Suite I,* 1991
Graphite and acrylic on canvas
94¹/₈ x 74³/₄ inches (239 x 190 cm)
Courtesy Sperone Westwater,
New York
Plate 24

27. *San Juan de la Cruz,* 1992
Mixed media on mattress
80 x 80 x 4 inches (203.2 x 203.2
x 10.2 cm)
Courtesy Sperone Westwater,
New York
Plate 23

28. *Untitled (People on Fire),* 1994
Acrylic on canvas
63¹/₄ x 67³/₄ inches (161 x 172 cm)
Collection of Donna and Howard
Stone, Chicago, courtesy Sperone
Westwater, New York

Jac Leirner

29. *Untitled (Corpus Delicti),* 1993
Forks, knives, and spoons from various
airlines, and polyurethane cord
125¹/₈ x 16 x 7¹/₈ inches (318 x 40.5
x 18 cm)
The Bohen Foundation
Plates 30 and 31

30. *Untitled (Corpus Delicti),*
1993/95
Luggage tags and wire
Dimensions vary with installation;
64 elements
Collection of the artist, courtesy
Galerie Lelong, New York
Plates 26 and 27

31. *Todos os Cem [All the One
Hundreds],* 1995
Brazilian currencies
Dimensions vary with installation;
3¹/₈ x 6⁵/₁₆ x 236¹/₄ inches diameter
(8 x 16 x 600 cm)
Collection of the artist, courtesy
Galerie Lelong, New York

Brice Marden

32. *The Sisters,* 1991–93
Oil on linen
84 x 59 inches (213.3 x 150 cm)
Private Collection, San Francisco
Plate 32

33. *Corpus,* 1992–94
Oil on linen
71 x 57 inches (180.3 x 145 cm)
Froehlich Collection, Stuttgart
Plate 34

34. *Second Body,* 1992–95
Oil on linen
71 x 57 inches (180.3 x 145 cm)
Collection of the artist, courtesy
Matthew Marks Gallery, New York

35. *Calcium,* 1992–95
Oil on linen
71 x 57 inches (180.3 x 145 cm)
Collection of the artist, courtesy
Matthew Marks Gallery, New York

36. *Progression,* 1992–95
Oil on linen
71 x 57 inches (180.3 x 145 cm)
Collection of the artist, courtesy
Matthew Marks Gallery, New York

Kerry James Marshall

37. *Better Homes Better Gardens,*
1994
Acrylic and collage on canvas
100 x 144 inches (254 x 366 cm)
Courtesy of the artist and Jack
Shainman Gallery, New York
Plate 37

38. *C.H.I.A.,* 1994
Acrylic and collage on canvas
120 x 114 inches (305 x 290 cm)
Courtesy of the artist and Koplin
Gallery, Santa Monica
Plate 36

39. *Many Mansions,* 1994
Acrylic and collage on canvas
114 x 135 inches (290 x 343 cm)
Courtesy of the artist and Koplin
Gallery, Santa Monica
Plate 35

40. *Untitled (Altgeld Gardens),* 1995
Acrylic and collage on canvas
78 x 100 inches (198 x 254 cm)
Courtesy of the artist and Jack
Shainman Gallery, New York

Doris Salcedo

41. *Atrabiliarios [Defiant],* 1994–95
Wall installation with plywood, shoes,
animal fiber, and surgical thread
Dimensions vary with installation;
37 niches varying in height from 9 to
13 inches (23 to 33 cm) and in width
from 3¹/₂ to 7 inches (9 to 18 cm) x
3¹/₂ inches (8.9 cm) deep installed;
with 30 skin boxes; each 7³/₄ x 15¹/₂ x
13 inches (20 x 40 x 33 cm)
Courtesy of the artist and Brooke
Alexander, New York

42. *La Casa Viuda VI [The Widowed
House VI],* 1995
Wood, fabric, plastic, and bone
Dimensions vary with installation
Courtesy of the artist and Brooke
Alexander, New York

Anna Deavere Smith

43. *Conversational Placements,* 1995
Conceived, written, and performed
by Anna Deavere Smith
Performance with sound and slide
projections
Presented by The Art Institute of
Chicago in association with The
Goodman Theatre

Barbara Steinman

44. *L'Ecoute [Gesture],* 1992
Two cibachrome pearl photographs
Each 67¹/₂ x 37³/₁₆ inches
(171.5 x 94.5 cm)
Edition 1/5
Collection of Alison and Alan
Schwartz
Plates 49 and 50

45. *Objects and Instruments,* 1992
Twenty-four inscribed lenses in brass
tripods
Dimensions vary with installation;
each tripod 33 x 24 inches diameter
at base (83.8 x 61 cm)
Courtesy of the artist and Olga Korper
Gallery, Toronto
Plate 48 and inset

Jeff Wall

46. *Coastal Motifs,* 1989
Cibachrome transparency, fluorescent
light, and display case
Image size: 46⁷/₈ x 57⁷/₈ inches
(119 x 147 cm)
Courtesy of the artist

47. *An Encounter in the Calle Valentín
Gómez Farías, Tijuana,* 1991
Cibachrome transparency, fluorescent
light, and display case
Image size: 90 x 113³/₈ inches
(229 x 288 cm)
Emanuel Hoffmann Foundation,
courtesy Museum für Gegenwarts-
kunst, Basel
Plates 52 and 53

48. *Fight on the Sidewalk,* 1994
Cibachrome transparency, fluorescent
light, and display case
Image size: 74³/₈ x 120⁷/₈ inches
(189 x 307 cm)
Collection of Jordi Soley, Barcelona
Plate 51

49. *Park Drive,* 1995
Cibachrome transparency, fluorescent
light, and display case
Image size: 46⁷/₈ x 53⁹/₁₆ inches
(119 x 136 cm)
Courtesy Marian Goodman Gallery,
New York

Andrea Zittel

50. *A–Z Management &
Maintenance Unit, Model 003,* 1992
Steel, wood, carpet, mirror, plastic
sink, stove top, and glass
86 x 94 x 68 inches (218.5 x 239 x
173 cm)
Collection of Andrea Rosen, New York

51. *A–Z 1994 Living Unit Customized
for Eileen and Peter Norton,* 1994
Wood, steel, and objects
57 x 82 x 82 inches (145 x 208 x
208 cm)
Collection of Eileen and Peter Norton,
Santa Monica

Vija Celmins
Born 1938, Riga, Latvia
Lives in New York

Education

1965 U.C.L.A., Los Angeles, MFA
1962 John Herron Institute, Indianapolis, BFA
1961 Yale University, New Haven, Connecticut, Summer Session, Fellowship

Selected Exhibitions

The rich range of exhibitions that punctuate Vija Celmins's thirty-year career highlights both the evolution of her art and the diversity of her style and media. Among numerous group exhibitions, her work has been included in such varied shows as "Thirteen Views of the West," Philadelphia Museum of Art (1966); "California Prints," The Museum of Modern Art, New York (1972); "American Drawings," Whitney Museum of American Art, New York (1973); "America 1976," Corcoran Gallery of Art, Washington, D.C. (traveling) (1976); "The Contemporary American Landscape," Hirschl and Adler Contemporary Art, New York (1981); "American Still Life 1945–1983," Contemporary Arts Museum, Houston (traveling) (1983–84); "American Women Artists Part I; 20th Century Pioneers," Sidney Janis Gallery, New York (1984); "Individuals: A Selected History of Contemporary Art, 1945–1986," The Museum of Contemporary Art, Los Angeles (1986–87); "L.A. Pop in the Sixties," Newport Harbor Art Museum, Newport Beach, California (traveling) (1989); "The Times. The Chronicle. and The Observer," Kent Fine Art, New York (1991); "Azur," Cartier Foundation, Paris (1993); and "Facts and Figures: Selections from the Lannan Foundation Collection," Lannan Foundation, Los Angeles (1994). Celmins's work has also been featured in a number of major survey exhibitions, including the "Annual of Contemporary American Sculpture," Whitney Museum of American Art, New York (1970); "Seventy-First American Exhibition," The Art Institute of Chicago (1974); and the "Biennial Exhibition," Whitney Museum of American Art (1977). Her solo exhibitions include an early show at the Whitney Museum of American Art, New York (1973); a mid-career survey, "Vija Celmins: A Survey Exhibition," organized by the Newport Harbor Art Museum, Newport Beach, California (traveling) (1980); shows at McKee Gallery, New York (1983, 1988, 1992); and most recently "Vija Celmins," organized by the Institute of Contemporary Art, Philadelphia, and traveling to the Walker Art Center, Minneapolis; the Whitney Museum of American Art, New York; and The Museum of Contemporary Art, Los Angeles (1992–94). Vija Celmins has received two Fellowships from the National Endowment for the Arts (1971, 1976) and a Guggenheim Fellowship (1980).

Selected Further Reading

Armstrong, Richard. "Of Earthly Objects and Stellar Sights: Vija Celmins." *Art in America* 69, 5 (May 1981), pp. 100–107.

Bartman, William S., ed. *Vija Celmins*. Los Angeles: A.R.T. Press. Interview by Chuck Close. 1992.

Los Angeles, Fellows of Contemporary Art. *Vija Celmins: A Survey Exhibition*. Text by Susan C. Larsen. Exh. cat. 1979.

Philadelphia, Institute of Contemporary Art. *Vija Celmins*. Organized by Judith Tannenbaum, with essays by Douglas Blau and Dave Hickey. Exh. cat. 1992.

Relyea, Lane. "Earth to Vija Celmins." *Artforum* 32, 2 (Oct. 1993), pp. 54–59.

Eugenio Dittborn
Born 1943, Santiago, Chile
Lives in Santiago

Education

1965–70 Studied in Paris, Madrid, West Berlin (Graphic Arts, Painting)
1962–65 School of Fine Arts, Universidad de Chile, Santiago (Engraving, Drawing, and Painting)

Selected Exhibitions

From the Chilean capital of Santiago where they originate, Eugenio Dittborn's Airmail Paintings have traveled via international post to exhibition venues worldwide. Since 1974 Dittborn's Airmail Paintings, in addition to his books, videos, and performances, have been featured in Latin American institutions from annual shows in his native Santiago to exhibitions in Bogotá, Pereira, and Cali, Colombia (1978, 1984, 1987), Rio de Janeiro (1984), Buenos Aires (1985), Lima (1988), and Caracas (1990). He has exhibited throughout Australia, Canada, and England, as well as in European venues in Amsterdam, Antwerp, Barcelona, Berlin, Cologne, Rome, and Rotterdam. In the United States, his work has been exhibited in New York, Boston, Washington, D.C., and Miami, and will premiere in Chicago with this exhibition. Dittborn's work has been featured in numerous international surveys, including "V Norwegian Graphic Arts Biennale," Oslo (1980); "Medellín Biennale," Medellín, Colombia (1981); "XII Paris Biennale" (1982); "5th Biennale of Sydney" (1984); "Latin American Triennale," Museum of Contemporary Hispanic Art, New York (1984, 1988); "Segunda Bienal Internacional de Pintura de Cuenca," Cuenca, Ecuador (1989); "Havana Biennale" (1989 and 1991); and "Documenta IX," Kassel (1992). Other significant exhibitions include "Transcontinental: Nine Latin American Artists," Ikon Gallery, Birmingham, and The Cornerhouse, Manchester, England (1990); "Latin American Artists of the Twentieth Century," The Museum of Modern Art, New York (traveling) (1992–93); "Out of Place," Vancouver Art Gallery (1993); and a retrospective, "MAPA: The Airmail Paintings of Eugenio Dittborn 1984–1992," Institute of Contemporary Arts, London, and Witte de With Center for Contemporary Art, Rotterdam (traveling) (1993). Eugenio Dittborn is the recipient of a Guggenheim Fellowship (1985).

Selected Further Reading

Brett, Guy and Sean Cubitt. *Camino Way*. Ed. Eugenio Dittborn. Santiago, Chile, 1991.

Cubitt, Sean. "Retrato Hablado: The Airmail Paintings of Eugenio Dittborn." *Third Text* 13 (Winter 1990–91), pp. 17–25.

London, Institute of Contemporary Arts, and Rotterdam, Witte de With Center for Contemporary Art. *Mapa: The Airmail Paintings of Eugenio Dittborn 1984–1992*. Contributions by Guy Brett, Sean Cubitt, Eugenio Dittborn, Roberto Merino, Gonzalo Muñoz, Nelly Richard, and Adriana Valdés. Exh. cat. 1993.

Miami, Center for the Fine Arts. *Eugenio Dittborn: In an Instant and with Devastating Fury, 4 New Airmail Paintings*. Essay by Louis Grachos. Exh. brochure. 1993.

Sydney, Artspace. *From Another Periphery: 10 Airmail Paintings*. Text by Adriana Valdés. Exh. brochure. 1984.

Leonardo Drew

Born 1961, Tallahassee, Florida
Lives in New York

Education

1982–85 The Cooper Union School for the Advancement of Science and Art, New York, BFA
1981–82 Parsons School of Design, New York

Selected Exhibitions

With formal complexity and use of such detritus as charred wooden slats and rusted metal in combination with cotton fabric and mortar, Leonardo Drew's large-scale sculptural assemblages powerfully merge the political, the personal, and the aesthetic. Simultaneously evoking African-American history and a rich artistic legacy, Drew's achievement has been recognized in exhibitions since 1974. Following a series of early solo exhibitions in Westport and Bridgeport, Connecticut, where he grew up, Drew's work was included in "Pillar to Post" at Kenkeleba House, New York (1985) and "Outside the Clock" at Scott Hansen Gallery, New York (1989). His work gained further attention during Drew's artist's residency at The Studio Museum in Harlem, New York (1991), where his work was included in "From the Studio: Artists in Residence, 1990–91" (1991). Since then, he has had solo exhibitions at Thread Waxing Space, New York (1992, 1994); the Herbert F. Johnson Museum of Art, Cornell University, Ithaca, New York (1994); Barbara Toll Fine Arts, New York (1994); and the Walter/McBean Gallery, San Francisco Art Institute (1994). He has participated in group shows at Nicole Klagsbrun Gallery, New York (1992); in "Three Sculptors: Leonardo Drew, Lisa Hoke, Brad Kahlhamer" at Thread Waxing Space, New York (1992); at Kunsthalle, New York (1992); in "Markets of Resistance" at White Columns, New York (1993); and in "Promising Suspects" at the Aldrich Museum of Contemporary Art, Ridgefield, Connecticut (1994). His work was also featured in "Biennial Dakar," Senegal, (1992). This is Leonardo Drew's first exhibition in Chicago.

Selected Further Reading

Als, Hilton. "Openings: Leonardo Drew." *Artforum* 6 (Feb. 1993), p. 94.

Glueck, Grace. "Three Favorite Exhibitions of 1992: Matisse, New York Museum of Modern Art; Magritte, Metropolitan Museum of Art; Leonardo Drew, Thread Waxing Space." *art* 1 (Jan. 1993), p. 104.

Heartney, Eleanor. "Leonardo Drew at Thread Waxing Space." *Art in America* 3 (Mar. 1993), pp. 112–113.

Cotter, Holland. "Art in Review: Leonardo Drew." *The New York Times*, April 1, 1994, Section C, p. 20.

New York, Thread Waxing Space. *Leonardo Drew*. Essay by Thomas McEvilley and interview by Tim Nye. Exh. cat. 1992.

Felix Gonzalez-Torres

Born 1957, Guáimaro, Cuba
Lives in New York

Education

1987 International Center for Photography, New York University, MFA
1983 Pratt Institute, Brooklyn, BFA
1983, 1981 Whitney Museum of American Art, New York, Independent Study Progam

Selected Exhibitions

Felix Gonzalez-Torres's billboards and light installations, paper stacks and candy piles, have offered his spectators quiet provocation, moments for contemplation, and generous invitations to literally take a piece of his work, demanding audience participation to impart meaning. Since 1987 Gonzalez-Torres has exhibited his work on city sidewalks and in museums and galleries around the world, in exhibitions that have disrupted traditional barriers between public and private, viewer and artwork. In a number of exhibitions, his public billboard installations have appeared in locations across Manhattan (1989, 1990, 1992); as well as in Los Angeles (1994); Milwaukee (1993); Graz, Austria (1992); and in Copenhagen, Cologne, Madrid, and Rome through "Paradise Europe" (1992). His work has also been the subject of numerous solo exhibitions in New York at The New Museum of Contemporary Art (1988); the Brooklyn Museum (1989); the Andrea Rosen Gallery (1990, 1991, 1992, 1993); and The Museum of Modern Art (1992); as well as in Europe at the Museum Fridericianum, Kassel (1991); Galerie Peter Pakesch, Vienna (1992); Magasin 3 Stockholm Konsthall, Stockholm (1992); and in Paris at Galerie Jennifer Flay (1993), Galerie Ghislaine Hussenot (1993), and the Musée d'art moderne de la ville de Paris (1993). In 1994 a major traveling show of his work was collaboratively organized and exhibited by The Museum of Contemporary Art, Los Angeles; the Hirshhorn Museum and Sculpture Garden, Washington, D.C.; and The Renaissance Society at the University of Chicago; and a retrospective, "Felix Gonzalez-Torres" at the Solomon R. Guggenheim Museum, New York (1995) is currently in progress. He has also been included in the "Biennial Exhibition," Whitney Museum of American Art (1991), and "Aperto 1993" in conjunction with "La Biennale di Venezia" (1993). Other notable venues include Fundación Caja de Pensiones, Madrid (1991); the Walker Art Center, Minneapolis (1992); the Wacoal Art Center, Tokyo (1992); Kunstverein, Hamburg, and Kunstmuseum Luzern (1992); the Institute of Contemporary Art, Philadelphia (1993); and the Camden Arts Center, London (1994). Gonzalez-Torres is the recipient of two Artists Fellowships from the National Endowment for the Arts (1989, 1993), a Gordon Matta-Clark Foundation Award (1991), and a Deutscher Akademischer Austauschdienst Fellowship (DAAD) (1992).

Selected Further Reading

Bartman, William S., ed. *Felix Gonzalez-Torres*. Los Angeles: A.R.T. Press. Essay by Susan Cahan, short story by Jan Avgikos, and interview with the artist by Tim Rollins. 1993.

Los Angeles, The Museum of Contemporary Art. *Felix Gonzalez-Torres*. Ed. Russell Ferguson, with essays by Amada Cruz, Russell Ferguson, Ann Goldstein, bell hooks, Joseph Kosuth, and Charles Merewether. Exh. cat. 1994.

Milwaukee, Milwaukee Art Museum. *Currents 22: Felix Gonzalez-Torres*. Essay by Dean Sobel. Exh. brochure. 1993.

New York, Solomon R. Guggenheim Museum. *Felix Gonzalez-Torres*. Text by Nancy Spector. Exh. cat. 1995.

Parkett 39 (Winter 1994). Special issue on Felix Gonzalez-Torres, with essays by Nancy Spector, Susan Tallman, and Simon Watney.

Rodney Graham
Born 1949, Matsqui, British Columbia, Canada
Lives in Vancouver

Education

1978–79 Simon Fraser University, Vancouver, Fine Arts Department
1968–72 University of British Columbia, Vancouver, Fine Arts Department

Selected Exhibitions

An interest in Romanticism's enduring legacy runs throughout Rodney Graham's diverse body of work. Since 1973 Graham's camera obscura photographs, architectural projects, music, and books have been exhibited widely throughout Canada and Europe, as well as in the United States, Australia, and Japan. In Canada his shows have included exhibitions at the Vancouver Art Gallery (1973, 1988 solo, 1991); Ydessa Gallery, Toronto (1987 solo); the Art Gallery of Ontario, Toronto (1987 solo); Walter Phillips Gallery, Banff (1988); and the Centre international d'art contemporain, Montreal (1990). In Europe he has had solo exhibitions at Galerie Johnen & Schöttle in Cologne (1986, 1988, 1990); Galerie Nelson, Lyon (1988, 1993); Stedelijk Van Abbemuseum, Eindhoven (1989); Galeria Marga Paz, Madrid (1989); Yves Gevaert, Brussels (1989, 1992); Galerie Micheline Szwajcer, Antwerp (1989, 1992); Galerie Rudiger Schöttle, Paris (1991); as well as Lisson Gallery, London (1990, 1993). In the United States, Graham's solo shows include Christine Burgin Gallery, New York (1988, 1990) and Angles Gallery, Santa Monica, California (1993). Graham has also participated in a number of significant European group shows, including "Kunst-Rai 1988," Amsterdam (1988); "Documenta IX," Kassel (1992); "La Biennale di Venezia" (1993); "Fokus: Canada 1960–1985," Cologne (1986); and "Time and Tide," Newcastle (1993). Other preeminent venues include the De Appel Foundation, Amsterdam (1987, 1992); Museum Haus Esters and Museum Haus Lange, Krefeld, Germany (1990–91); Crousel-Robelin, Paris (1991); Kunstmuseum Winterthur, Switzerland (1992); and Musée Communal d'Ixeliès, Brussels (1992).

Selected Further Reading

Barcelona, Centre d'Art Santa Mònica. *Càmeres Indiscretes*. Essays by José Lebrero Stals et al. Exh. cat. 1992.

Getigne-Clisson, France, FRAC des Pays de la Loire. *Canada: une nouvelle génération*. Organized by Anne Dary. Essays by Catherine Bédard and Marc Mayer. Exh. cat. 1993.

Linsley, Robert. "In Pursuit of the Vanishing Subject: James Welling and Rodney Graham." *C Magazine* 18 (Winter 1987), pp. 26–29.

North York, Ontario, Art Gallery of York University. *Rodney Graham*. Essays by Marie Ange Brayer et al. 1994.

Wall, Jeff. "Into the Forest: Two Sketches for Studies of Rodney Graham's Work." In Vancouver, Vancouver Art Gallery. *Rodney Graham*. Exh. cat. 1988.

Ann Hamilton
Born 1956, Lima, Ohio
Lives in Columbus

Education

1985 Yale School of Art, New Haven, Connecticut, MFA in Sculpture
1979 University of Kansas, Kansas City, BFA in Textile Design
1974–76 St. Lawrence University, Canton, New York

Selected Exhibitions

Ann Hamilton's name has been at the forefront of installation art for close to a decade. For Hamilton, the specific locale or exhibition site frequently becomes an integral component of the final work, lending a unique significance to her exhibition geography. Within the United States, she has shown in numerous venues from coast to coast, and early on showed widely in California, where her work has been featured at the Santa Barbara Contemporary Arts Forum (1985); The Museum of Contemporary Art, Los Angeles (1988); Capp Street Project, San Francisco (1989); and the San Diego Museum of Contemporary Art, La Jolla (1990). Additionally, she has had solo exhibitions at the Hirshhorn Museum and Sculpture Garden, Washington, D.C. (1991); MIT List Visual Art Center, Cambridge, Mass. (1992); Walker Art Center, Minneapolis (1992); Henry Art Gallery, University of Washington, Seattle (1992); Dia Center for the Arts, New York (1993); Power Plant, Toronto (1993); Tate Gallery Liverpool (1994); and The Museum of Modern Art, New York (1994). She has participated in a number of significant group exhibitions, such as the "Carnegie International 1991," The Carnegie Museum of Art, Pittsburgh (1991); "Places with a Past: New Site-Specific Art at Charleston's Spoleto Festival" (1991); and "Dirt & Domesticity: Constructions of the Feminine," at the Whitney Museum of American Art, New York (1992). Hamilton's work has been widely shown internationally as well. She represented America at the "Bienal Internacional de São Paulo" (1991); participated in "Sonsbeek 93" in Arnhem, Holland (1993); and has shown work at The National Museum of Modern Art in Kyoto (1990); the Fundación Caja de Pensiones in Madrid (1991); Hayward Gallery in London (1992); and Kunsthalle Wien in Vienna (1993). Hamilton has been commissioned to create permanent projects for the Headlands Center for the Arts in Sausalito, California (1989–90) and for the San Francisco Public Library (1990–93). Among numerous awards, Ann Hamilton has received a Guggenheim Fellowship (1989), a Louis Comfort Tiffany Foundation Award (1990), a MacArthur Fellowship (1993) and a National Endowment for the Arts Fellowship (1993).

Selected Further Reading

Seattle, Henry Gallery Association. *Ann Hamilton: 21st International Bienal of São Paulo*. Essay by Joan Hugo. Exh. cat. 1991.

Jacob, Mary Jane, and Theodore Rosengarten. *Places with a Past: New Site-Specific Art at Charleston's Spoleto Festival*. Exh. cat. New York: Rizzoli International Publications, Inc., 1991.

La Jolla, California, San Diego Museum of Contemporary Art. *Ann Hamilton*. Essay by Susan Stewart. Exh. cat. 1991.

Liverpool, England, Tate Gallery Liverpool. *Ann Hamilton: mneme*. Essays by Neville Wakefield and Judith Nesbitt. Exh. cat. 1994.

Seattle, The Henry Art Gallery, University of Washington. *Ann Hamilton: São Paulo/Seattle*. Essays by Chris Bruce and Buzz Spector. Exh. cat. 1992.

Larry Johnson

Born 1959, Long Beach, California
Lives in Los Angeles

Selected Exhibitions

The caustic vernacular vision that identifies Larry Johnson's distinctly West Coast text-scapes has been explored in numerous exhibitions in the United States and abroad. Not surprisingly, his work has provided rich fodder for the past decade's outcropping of shows on postmodern uses of language, and the legacy of California art. He was featured in "CalArts: Skeptical Belief(s)," The Renaissance Society at the University of Chicago and Newport Harbor Art Museum, Newport Beach, California (1987); "Modes of Address: 25 Years of Language in Art," Whitney Museum of American Art at Federal Reserve Plaza, New York (1988); "Utopia Post Utopia," the Institute of Contemporary Art, Boston (1988); "A Forest of Signs," The Museum of Contemporary Art, Los Angeles (1989); "Image World," Whitney Museum of American Art, New York (1989); "Word as Image: American Art 1960–1990," Milwaukee Art Museum (traveling) (1990); "True Stories," Institute of Contemporary Arts, London (1992); "Die Sprache der Kunst (The Language of Art)" Kunsthalle, Vienna (1993) and Kunstverein, Frankfurt (1994); and "Love in the Ruins: Art and the Inspiration of L.A.," Long Beach Museum of Art, California (1994). His work has also been included in a number of significant recent photography exhibitions, including "California Photography: Remaking Make Believe," The Museum of Modern Art, New York (traveling) (1989); "The Photography of Invention," National Museum of Art, Smithsonian Institution, Washington, D.C. (traveling) (1989); "The Indomitable Spirit," International Center of Photography, New York (1990); and "A Dialogue About Recent American and European Photography," The Museum of Contemporary Art, Los Angeles (1991). Larry Johnson has also been included in several biennials; "Documenta 8," Kassel (1987); "Aperto 88," in conjunction with "La Biennale di Venezia" (1988); and the "Biennial Exhibition," Whitney Museum of American Art, New York (1991). His work has been the subject of solo shows at 303 Gallery, New York (1986, 1987, 1989, 1990, 1991); Stuart Regen Gallery, Los Angeles (1990); Rena Bransten Gallery, San Francisco (1991); and Margo Leavin Gallery, Los Angeles (1994), as well as at European galleries in Stuttgart, Milan, Cologne, Paris, and Bruges, Belgium, since 1987.

Selected Further Reading

Goldstein, Ann. "Dialogues and Accidence." In Los Angeles, The Museum of Contemporary Art. *A Dialogue About Recent American and European Photography*. Exh. cat. 1991.

Hickey, Dave. "Larry Johnson's Malicious Muzak." *Frieze* 14 (Jan./Feb. 1994), cover and pp. 30–35.

Los Angeles, The Museum of Contemporary Art. *A Forest of Signs: Art in the Crisis of Representation*. Essays by Ann Goldstein, Mary Jane Jacob, Anne Rorimer, and Howard Singerman. Exh. cat. 1989.

Myers, Terry R. "Hard Copy: The Sincerely Fraudulent Photographs of Larry Johnson." *Arts Magazine* 65, 10 (Summer 1991), pp. 40–45.

Pagel, David. "Larry Johnson at Stuart Regen." *Art Issues* 16 (Feb./Mar. 1991), pp. 38–39.

Guillermo Kuitca

Born 1961, Buenos Aires, Argentina
Lives in Buenos Aires

Selected Exhibitions

Guillermo Kuitca had his first solo exhibition at age thirteen and has continued to exhibit his paintings of maps, plans, and genealogical charts at a precocious pace ever since. In the twenty years since his debut at Galeria Lirolay in Buenos Aires (1974), Kuitca's work has been featured in solo and group exhibitions worldwide. He has been the subject of one-person exhibitions at Thomas Cohn Arte Contemporanea, Rio de Janeiro (1986, 1989, 1994); Witte de With Center for Contemporary Art, Rotterdam (1990); Kunsthalle Basel (1990); The Museum of Modern Art, New York (traveling) (1991–92); Musée d'art contemporain de Montréal (1993); IVAM Centre del Carme en Valencia (traveling) (1993–94); Sperone Westwater, New York (1994); and "Burning Beds: Guillermo Kuitca, A Survey 1982–1994" at the Wexner Center for the Arts, Columbus, Ohio (traveling) (1994–95). Highlights among Kuitca's many international group shows include "Intergrafik 83," Berlin (1983); "Bienal Internacional de São Paulo" (1985, 1989); "Documenta IX," Kassel (1992); and "La Biennale di Venezia" (1993). His work has also been featured at the Museo de Arte Moderno, Buenos Aires (1980, 1981, 1983); in "U-ABC" at Amsterdam's Stedelijk Museum (1989); "Currents 1992: The Absent Body," at the Institute of Contemporary Art, Boston (1992); "Latin American Artists of the Twentieth Century," The Museum of Modern Art, New York (traveling) (1992–93); "Cartographies—14 Artists from Latin America," The Winnipeg Art Gallery, Manitoba (traveling) (1993–94); "Art on the Map," Chicago Cultural Center (1994); "La Ville," Musée national d'art moderne, Centre Georges Pompidou, Paris (1994); and "Mapping," at The Museum of Modern Art, New York (1994).

Selected Further Reading

Amsterdam, Contemporary Art Foundation Amsterdam. *A Book Based on Guillermo Kuitca*. Essays by Jerry Saltz, Martin Rejtman, and Marcelo E. Pacheco. 1993.

New York, Contemporary Art Foundation Amsterdam. *Guillermo Kuitca–Burning Beds, A Survey 1982–1994*. Essays by Lynne Cooke et al. Exh. cat. 1994.

New York, The Museum of Modern Art. *Guillermo Kuitca/Projects 30*. Essay by Lynn Zelevansky. Exh. brochure. 1991.

Rome, Gian Enzo Sperone, in collaboration with Annina Nosei Gallery, New York. *Guillermo Kuitca*. Text by Charles Merewether. Exh. cat. 1990.

Rotterdam, Witte de With Center for Contemporary Art. *Guillermo Kuitca*. Text by Rina Carvajal and Chris Dercon. Exh. cat. 1990.

Jac Leirner
Born 1961, São Paulo, Brazil
Lives in São Paulo

Education

1979–84 College of Fine Arts, Armando Alvares Penteado Foundation, São Paulo

Selected Exhibitions

For more than a decade, Jac Leirner's work has reflected her own artistic itinerary. Located as she is in Brazil, Leirner's frequent transcontinental travels from São Paulo to exhibition venues worldwide have been both a practical and a creative necessity, as the primary means through which she gathers materials to compose her elegant post-Minimalist sculptures. In addition to a series of solo shows in her native São Paulo, most recently at Galeria Camargo Vilaca (1993), she has had one-person exhibitions in the United States at the Institute of Contemporary Art, Boston (1991); the Walker Art Center, Minneapolis, where she was an artist in residence (1991); the Hirshhorn Museum and Sculpture Garden, Washington, D.C. (1992); and at Galerie Lelong, New York (1994). In Europe she has had solo shows at the Museum of Modern Art, Oxford, as an artist in residence there (1991); Galerie Hoffmann, Friedberg, Germany (1992); and the Centre d'Art Contemporain, Geneva (1993). Her work has been featured in the "Bienal Internacional de São Paulo" (1983, 1989, 1994); the "Cali Biennale of Graphic Arts," Colombia (1986); "Aperto '90" in conjunction with "La Biennale di Venezia" (1990); and "Documenta IX," Kassel (1992). Leirner has participated in other major international group shows, including "Art in the Streets I," "The New Dimension of the Object," and "A Presenca do Ready-made, 80 anos," all at The Museum of Contemporary Art, São Paulo (1983, 1986, and 1993, respectively); "Transcontinental: Nine Latin American Artists" at Ikon Gallery, Birmingham, and the Cornerhouse, Manchester, England (1990); "TransMission" at Rooseum Center for Contemporary Art, Malmö, Sweden (1991); "Past Future Tense," Vancouver Art Gallery (traveling) (1991); "Latin American Artists of the Twentieth Century," The Museum of Modern Art, New York (traveling) (1992); "Sense and Sensibility: Women Artists and Minimalism in the 90s," The Museum of Modern Art, New York (1994); and currently "Latin American Women Artists, 1915–1995" at the Milwaukee Art Museum. Leirner has also exhibited in Bogotá, Cologne, Paris, Stockholm, Tokyo, Vancouver, and Winnipeg.

Selected Further Reading

Brett, Guy. *Transcontinental: Nine Latin American Artists*. London, Verso, in association with Ikon Gallery, Birmingham, and The Cornerhouse, Manchester. Additional texts by the artists, Lu Menezes, and Paulo Venancio Filho. Exh. cat. 1990.

Cruz, Amada. "Jac Leirner." In Washington, D.C., Hirshhorn Museum and Sculpture Garden, Smithsonian Institution. *Directions*. Exh. brochure. 1993.

Ferguson, Bruce W. "Jac Leirner: Short Circuits and Mini-Systems." In Minneapolis, Walker Art Center. *Viewpoints*. Exh. brochure. 1991.

Oxford, Museum of Modern Art. *Jac Leirner*. Essay by David Elliott. Exh. cat. 1991.

Sullivan, Edward J. "Fantastic Voyage: Latin American Explosion." *Artnews* 92, 6 (Summer 1993), pp. 140–41.

Brice Marden
Born 1938, Bronxville, New York
Lives in New York

Education

1963 Yale University School of Art and Architecture, New Haven, Connecticut, MFA
1961 Boston University School of Fine and Applied Arts, BFA

Selected Exhibitions

For more than thirty years, Brice Marden's paintings, drawings, and prints have profoundly and originally advanced the terms of American abstraction for international audiences. His celebrated work has been the subject of sixty-eight solo exhibitions at museums and galleries, including three major traveling retrospectives. In 1991 "Brice Marden—Cold Mountain" originated at the Dia Center for the Arts, New York, and traveled to the Walker Art Center, Minneapolis; The Menil Collection, Houston; Museo Nacional Centro de Arte Reina Sofia, Madrid; and Kunstmuseum, Bonn. Additionally, his work was recently featured in "Brice Marden: Prints 1961–91," at Tate Gallery, London; the Musée d'art moderne de la ville de Paris; and The Baltimore Museum of Art (1991); "Brice Marden," at Museum für Gegenwartskunst, Basel, and Museum Fridericianum, Kassel (1993); and "Brice Marden: Painting since 1986" at Kunsthalle, Bern; Vienna Secession; and the Stedelijk Museum, Amsterdam (1993). Marden has had other notable solo shows at the Solomon R. Guggenheim Museum, New York (1975); the Stedelijk Museum, Amsterdam (1981); Whitechapel Art Gallery and Anthony d'Offay in London (1981, 1988); Michael Werner, Cologne (1989); and "Brice Marden: New Paintings, Drawings and Etchings" at Matthew Marks Gallery, New York (1993). Among Marden's more than 100 group exhibitions are the "1969 Annual Exhibition: Contemporary American Painting," Whitney Museum of American Art, New York (1969); "Prospect '69," and "Prospect '73 Maler, Painters, Peintres," Stadtische Kunsthalle, Düsseldorf (1969, 1973); the "Biennial Exhibition," Whitney Museum of American Art, New York (1973, 1977, 1989); the "Seventieth American Exhibition," The Art Institute of Chicago (1972); "Documenta 5," and "Documenta IX," Kassel (1972, 1992), and "Carnegie International," The Carnegie Museum of Art, Pittsburgh (1985). Other significant group shows include "White on White: The White Monochrome in the 20th Century," Museum of Contemporary Art, Chicago (1972); "A New Spirit in Painting," Royal Academy of Arts, London (1981); "Minimalism to Expressionism," Whitney Museum of American Art, New York (1986); "The Spiritual in Art: Abstract Painting 1890–1985," Los Angeles County Museum of Art (traveling) (1986); "Europa/Amerika," Ludwig Museum, Cologne (traveling) (1986); "Polyptiques," Musée du Louvre, Paris (1990); "Allegories of Modernism: Contemporary Drawing," The Museum of Modern Art, New York (1992); and "American Art in the 20th Century," Martin-Gropius-Bau, Berlin (traveling) (1993).

Selected Further Reading

Bois, Yve-Alain. "Marden's Doubt." In Bern, Kunsthalle. *Brice Marden: Paintings 1985–1993*. Exh. cat. 1993.

Boston, Museum of Fine Arts. *Brice Marden: Boston*. Text by Trevor Fairbrother, with contributions by Robert Creeley, Brice Marden, Patti Smith, and John Yau. Exh. cat. 1991.

Kertess, Klaus. *Brice Marden: Paintings and Drawings*. New York: Harry N. Abrams, 1992.

London, Tate Gallery. *Brice Marden: Prints 1961–1991*. Text by Jeremy Lewison. Exh. cat. 1992.

Richardson, Brenda. *Brice Marden Cold Mountain*. Houston: Houston Fine Arts Press, 1992.

Kerry James Marshall

Born 1955, Birmingham, Alabama
Lives in Chicago

Education

1978 Otis Art Institute, Los Angeles, BFA

Selected Exhibitions

Kerry James Marshall's career began fifteen years ago in California, where he first exhibited his vibrant narrative tableaux depicting African-American life and culture. He exhibited his paintings at university galleries there, including California State University in Dominguez Hills and Los Angeles (1980, 1984); Pepperdine University in Malibu (1984); Loyola Law School, Los Angeles (1985); and San Diego State University (1992). Marshall's early gallery exhibitions include both solo and group shows at a number of Los Angeles venues: Municipal Art Gallery (1979, 1986), Jan Baum Gallery (1980), James Turcotte Gallery (1983 solo), Koplin Gallery (1984, 1985 solo, 1991 solo, 1993 solo), and Brockman Gallery (1985). More recently he has exhibited at New York galleries, including Ledisflam (1993), White Columns (1993), Jack Shainman (1993 solo), Sonnabend Gallery (1994), and at Zolla/Lieberman Gallery in Chicago (1993). His work was featured in a solo exhibition at The Studio Museum in Harlem, New York (1986) during his tenure there as an artist in residence, and in a two-person exhibition with Santiago Vaca at the Chicago Cultural Center (1992). His most recent solo show, "Kerry James Marshall: Telling Stories: Selected Paintings," is traveling to venues in Cleveland; Overland Park, Kansas; St. Louis; and Pittsburgh. Marshall's notable group exhibitions include the "43rd Biennial Exhibition of Contemporary Painting" at the Corcoran Gallery of Art, Washington, D.C. (1993); "The Studio Museum in Harlem: 25 Years of African American Art," at the Paine Webber Art Gallery, New York (1993); "Bridges and Boundaries, Chicago Crossings," at the Spertus Museum, Chicago (1994); and "Korrespondenzen/Correspondences: Fourteen Artists from Berlin and Chicago," at the Berlinische Galerie, Museum für Moderne Kunst, Photographie, und Architektur in Berlin and the Chicago Cultural Center (1994–95).

Selected Further Reading

Berlin, Berlinische Galerie and Chicago, Chicago Cultural Center. *Korrespondenzen/Correspondences: Fourteen Artists from Berlin and Chicago.* Essays by Ursula Prinz, Gregory G. Knight, Judith Russi Kirshner. Entry by Arthur Jafa and Kerry James Marshall. Exh. cat. 1994.

Cleveland, Cleveland Center for Contemporary Art, and Pittsburgh, Pittsburgh Center for the Arts, *Kerry James Marshall: Telling Stories: Selected Paintings.* Essay by Terrie Sultan. Exh. cat. 1994.

Washington, D.C., Corcoran Gallery of Art. *43rd Biennial Exhibition of Contemporary Painting.* Organized by Terrie Sultan. Essay on Kerry James Marshall by David Pagel. Exh. cat. 1993.

Westfall, Stephen. "Kerry James Marshall at Jack Shainman." *Art in America* 81, 10 (Oct. 1993), p. 133.

Yau, John. "Kerry Marshall at Jack Shainman Gallery." *Artforum* 31, 9 (May 1993), pp. 106–107.

Doris Salcedo

Born 1958, Bogotá, Colombia
Lives in Bogotá

Education

1984 New York University, MFA in Sculpture
1980 Universidad de Bogotá Jorge Tadeo Lozano, BFA

Selected Exhibitions

Doris Salcedo's viscerally moving sculptures and installations—meditations on the violence and loss in her native Bogotá—were first exhibited publicly in 1990. In the brief time since, her work has garnered international acclaim through a growing list of exhibitions. She has had solo exhibitions at Casa de la Moneda (1985) and Galería Garcés-Velásquez in Bogotá (1990); the Shedhalle in Zurich (1992); and Brooke Alexander, New York (1994). She has been included in the "XXXI Annual Exhibition of Colombian Artists" in Colcultura, Medellín, Colombia (1992); the "Americas: Expo 1992," Seville (1992); the "9th Biennale of Sydney" (1992); and "Aperto 93" in conjunction with the "La Biennale di Venezia" (1993). Her work has been featured in other significant group exhibitions: several shows at Biblioteca Luis-Ángel Arango in Bogotá, including "Ante América" (traveling) (1992, 1993–94); "The Absent Body" at the Institute of Contemporary Art, Boston (1992); "Building a Collection" at the Museum of Fine Arts, Boston (1993); "The Spine" at the Foundation De Appel, Amsterdam (1994); and "Cocido y Crudo" at the Museo Nacional Centro de Arte Reina Sofia, Madrid (1994). In addition to several group shows at Brooke Alexander, New York (1993, 1994), she has also exhibited at Rhona Hoffman Gallery, Chicago (1994) and at John Berggruen in San Francisco (1994).

Selected Further Reading

Bogotá, Biblioteca Luis-Ángel Arango. *Ante América.* Ed. Carolina Ponce de Leon, with essays by Charles Merewether, Gerardo Mosquera, and Rachel Weiss. Exh. cat. 1992.

Cameron, Dan. "Absence Makes the Art: Doris Salcedo." *Artforum* 33, 2 (Oct. 1994), pp. 88–91.

Krebs, Edith. "The Power of the Norm: Children, Artists, and Other Delinquents." In Zurich, Shedhalle. *Doris Salcedo.* 1993.

Merewether, Charles. "Naming Violence in the Work of Doris Salcedo." *Third Text* 24 (1993), pp. 35–44.

Ponce de León, Carolina. "Acciones de Duelo." *El Tiempo* (Bogotá), May 12, 1990.

Anna Deavere Smith
Born 1950, Baltimore, Maryland
Lives in San Francisco

Education

1993 Beaver College, Glenside, PA, Honorary Doctorate
1976 American Conservatory Theater, San Francisco, MFA
1971 Beaver College, Glenside, Pennsylvania, BA in Linguistics

Actress and playwright Anna Deavere Smith has acted both on and off Broadway, regionally, and in film and television. *Twilight: Los Angeles, 1992* and *Fires in the Mirror: Crown Heights, Brooklyn and Other Identities* are part of a series, for which Smith is the author and performer, called *On the Road: A Search for American Character*. Smith first performed *Fires in the Mirror* at the Joseph Papp Public Theater in New York (1992). The tour (1993) included performances at the Arena Stage, Washington, D.C.; the Long Wharf Theatre, New Haven, Connecticut; the Royal Court Theatre, London; the Brooklyn Academy of Music, New York; the American Repertory Theatre, Cambridge, Massachussetts; The English Institute, Boston; McCarter Theatre, Princeton, New Jersey; and Berkeley Repertory Theatre, California. The American Playhouse version ran on PBS stations across the country to wide critical acclaim (1994). *Twilight: Los Angeles, 1992* was originally produced by the Center Theatre Group/Mark Taper Forum in Los Angeles (1993). It premiered in New York at the New York Shakespeare Festival/Joseph Papp Public Theater (1994) under the direction of George C. Wolfe, followed by a move to Broadway's Cort Theatre. Smith's play *Piano*, produced at the Los Angeles Theatre Center, received the 1991 Drama-Logue Award for Playwrighting. Smith has appeared on the "Arsenio Hall Show," and in the feature films *Dave* and *Philadelphia*. *On The Road: A Search for American Character* includes pieces created for the Eureka Theatre of San Francisco (*From the Outside Looking in: San Francisco, 1990*); the Rockefeller Center, Bellagio, Italy (*Fragments: On Intercultural Performance*); and Princeton University, New Jersey (*Gender Bending*). She collaborated with Judith Jamison on *Hymn*, a ballet for the 35th Anniversary Season of the Alvin Ailey American Dance Theatre, presented at City Center in New York (1993). Smith has received two Obie Awards, a Drama Desk Award, a New York Drama Critics Circle Award, two NAACP Theater Awards, The Lucille Lortel Award, the George and Elisabeth Marton Award, The Kesselring Prize, two Tony Award nominations for *Twilight: Los Angeles, 1992*, and she was a runner-up for the Pulitzer Prize in Drama for *Fires in the Mirror: Crown Heights, Brooklyn and Other Identities*. Anna Deavere Smith is the Ann O'Day Maples Professor of the Arts at Stanford University in Palo Alto, California.

Selected Further Reading

Kroll, Jack. "Fire in the City of Angels." *Newsweek* (June 28, 1993), pp. 62–63.

Lahr, John. "Under the Skin." *The New Yorker* (June 28, 1993), pp. 90–94.

Scasserra, Michael P. "Anna Deavere Smith: Woman of Many Colors." *Theater Week* (Mar. 28, 1994), pp. 19–27.

_____. "Embodiment of Diversity." *Performing Arts* (July 1993), pp. 36–45.

Stayton, Richard. "A Fire in a Crowded Theater." *American Theater* (July–Aug. 1993), pp. 22–25, 72–75.

Barbara Steinman
Born 1951, Montreal, Quebec, Canada
Lives in Montreal

Education

1972–74 Concordia University, Montreal, Masters Programme Communications
1968–71 McGill University, Montreal, BA in Literature

Selected Exhibitions

From numerous venues in her native Montreal to points throughout Canada and as far as Japan, Barbara Steinman has exhibited her politically charged multimedia installations and video work widely since 1980. In Canada she has exhibited in every province and major city, including solo shows at The National Gallery of Canada, Ottawa (1988); Galerie René Blouin, Montreal (1989, 1991, 1992); MacKenzie Art Gallery, Regina (1992); The Art Gallery of Windsor (1993); and Olga Korper Gallery, Toronto (1994). Her Canadian group show venues include the Vancouver Art Gallery (1983); the Centre international d'art contemporain de Montréal (1986, 1989, 1992); the Musée d'art contemporain de Montréal (1980, 1984, 1992); and The Art Gallery of Ontario, Toronto (1993). She has participated in the "19a Bienal Internacional de São Paulo" (1987); "Aperto '88" in conjunction with "La Biennale di Venezia" (1988); the "Fukui International Video Biennale," Japan (1988); the "Canadian Biennial of Contemporary Art," The National Gallery of Canada, Ottawa (1989); the "8th Biennale of Sydney" (1990); and the "Bienal de la Imagen en Movimiento '90" in Madrid (1990). Steinman's work has been exhibited at other international venues: the Espace Lyonnais d'art contemporain (ELAC) and the Hara Museum of Contemporary Art in Tokyo (1985); at FRAC des Pays de la Loire, Getigne-Clisson, France (1993); and Tate Gallery, Liverpool (1993). In the United States, she has shown at The New Museum of Contemporary Art, New York (1990); the International Sculpture Center, Washington, D.C. (1990); The Museum of Modern Art, New York (1990 project); the "Spoleto Festival U.S.A." in Charleston, South Carolina (1991); and The Jewish Museum, New York (1993). This exhibition marks Steinman's first appearance in Chicago.

Selected Further Reading

Ferguson, Bruce W. "The Art of Memory—Barbara Steinman." *Vanguard* 18, 3 (Summer 1989), cover and pp. 1–15.

Jacob, Mary Jane, and Theodore Rosengarten. *Places with a Past: New Site-Specific Art at Charleston's Spoleto Festival.* New York: Rizzoli International Publications, Inc. Exh. cat. 1991.

Regina, MacKenzie Art Gallery. *Barbara Steinman: Uncertain Monuments.* Introduction by Cindy Richmond and essay by Barbara London. Exh. cat. 1993.

Toronto, The Art Gallery of Ontario. *Positionings/Transpositions: Mona Hatoum & Barbara Steinman.* Essay by Michèle Thériault. Exh. cat. 1993.

Windsor, Ontario, Art Gallery of Windsor. *Barbara Steinman: A Lapse in Logic.* Essay by Reesa Greenberg. Exh. cat. 1994.

Jeff Wall

Born 1946, Vancouver, British Columbia, Canada
Lives in Vancouver

Selected Exhibitions

Merging art history and cinematography, Jeff Wall's large-scale cibachrome transparencies have shed new light on old forms, in exhibitions around the world for twenty years. His solo shows include The Renaissance Society at the University of Chicago (1983); the Institute of Contemporary Arts, London, and Kunsthalle, Basel (1984); Galerie Johnen & Schöttle, Cologne (1986, 1987, 1988, 1994); Museum für Gegenwartskunst, Basel (1987); Marian Goodman Gallery, New York (1989, 1990, 1992); Vancouver Art Gallery (1990); San Diego Museum of Contemporary Art, La Jolla, California (1992); the Palais des Beaux-Arts, Brussels (1992); Kunstmuseum Luzern (1993); Stadtische Kunsthalle, Düsseldorf (1994); the De Pont Foundation for Contemporary Art, Tilburg, The Netherlands (1994); and Museo Nacional Centro de Art Reina Sofia, Madrid (1994). Among the many notable group shows in which he has participated are "Information," The Museum of Modern Art, New York (1970); "Directions 1981," Hirshhorn Museum and Sculpture Garden, Washington, D.C. (1981); "Difference: On Representation and Sexuality," The New Museum of Contemporary Art, New York (traveling)(1984); "Utopia Post Utopia," Institute of Contemporary Art, Boston (1988); "Les Magiciens de la Terre," Musée national d'art moderne, Centre Georges Pompidou, Paris (1989); "Weitersehen 1980–1990," Museum Haus Lange and Museum Haus Esters, Krefeld, Germany (1990); "Passages de l'Image," Musée national d'art moderne, Centre Georges Pompidou, Paris (1990); "Post-Human," at the Deichtorhallen, Hamburg (1993); and "The Epic and the Everyday," Hayward Gallery, London (1994). His work has also been exhibited at "Documenta 7" and "8," Kassel (1982, 1987); "La Nouvelle Biennale de Paris" (1985); "Prospect 86," Frankfurt (1986); "Carnegie International," The Carnegie Museum of Art, Pittsburgh (1988); and the "7th Biennale of Sydney" (1988).

Selected Further Reading

Barents, Els. *Jeff Wall: Transparencies*. New York: Rizzoli International, 1987.

Guilbaut, Serge, ed. "Jeff Wall: Three Excerpts from a Discussion with T. J. Clark, Claude Gintz, Serge Guilbaut, and Anne Wagner." *Parkett* 22 (1989), pp. 82–85.

Kirshner, Judith. "A Blinding Art." *Real Life Magazine* (Winter 1983–84), pp. 40–42.

Lucerne, Kunstmuseum Luzern. *Dead Troops Talk*. Essay by Terry Atkinson. Exh. cat. 1993.

Vancouver, Vancouver Art Gallery. *Jeff Wall 1990*. Essays by Gary DuFour and Jerry Zaslove. Exh. cat. 1990.

Andrea Zittel

Born 1965, Escondido, California
Lives in Brooklyn, New York

Education

1990 Rhode Island School of Design, Providence, MFA in Sculpture
1988 San Diego State University, BFA in Painting and Sculpture (Honors)

Selected Exhibitions

In the brief five years since Andrea Zittel emerged on the New York art scene, her highly original artistic vision and bold "designs for living" have been recognized internationally in an impressive roster of exhibitions. Her young career has been marked by solo exhibitions at galleries including Jack Hanley Gallery, San Francisco (1993); Christopher Grimes Gallery, Santa Monica (1993); Andrea Rosen Gallery, New York (1993); and Anthony d'Offay Gallery, London (1994), as well as at The Carnegie Museum of Art in Pittsburgh (1994). Zittel's work has also been featured in several notable European group shows: Galerie Monica Spruth in Cologne (1993); "Real Time" at the Institute of Contemporary Arts, London (1993); "Aperto 1993" in conjunction with "La Biennale di Venezia" (1993); "L'hiver de l'amour," at the Musée d'art moderne de la ville de Paris (1994); Galerie Jennifer Flay, Paris (1994); and Kasper König's "Sammlung Volkmann" in Berlin (1994). Other European venues include shows at Massimo de Carlo, Milan (1993); Grazer Kunstverein and Neue Galerie in Graz, Austria (1994); and Manes, Prague (1994). Zittel's work has been exhibited widely in New York at such venues as Artist's Space (1991); Blum Helman Warehouse (1991); 303 Gallery (1992); the New Museum of Contemporary Art (1993); Thread Waxing Space (1994); and most recently in "Sense and Sensibility: Women Artists and Minimalism in the Nineties," at The Museum of Modern Art (1994). Andrea Zittel is a recipient of a Deutschen Akademischen Austauschdienst (DAAD) grant.

Selected Further Reading

Armstrong, Richard. "Three Living Systems." In Pittsburgh, The Carnegie Museum of Art. *Forum*. Exh. brochure. 1994.

Avikgos, Jan. "Sense and Sensibility: Museum of Modern Art." *Artforum* 33, 2 (Oct. 1994), pp. 98–99.

Saltz, Jerry. "Andrea Zittel at Andrea Rosen." *Art in America* 82, 6 (June 1994), pp. 100–101.

Weil, Benjamin. "Ouverture: Andrea Zittel." *Flash Art* 68 (Jan./Feb. 1993), p. 80.

New York, The Museum of Modern Art. *Sense and Sensibility: Women Artists and Minimalism in the Nineties*. Essay by Lynn Zelevansky. Exh. cat. 1993.

Acknowledgments

A project of this size and scope could not have been achieved without the enlightened interest and generous support of several agencies. I am grateful to the Bohen Foundation for its pivotal and very generous support of this exhibition in its earliest stages. I am particularly indebted to Frederick B. Henry, President of the Bohen Foundation, whose enthusiastic interest is acknowledged with profound appreciation, and also to Linda Cucchiara Behr and Kathleen Merrill. For their handsome grant I wish to thank AT&T, in particular Susan Atteridge and Dorothy Foster, for enabling us to expand our educational and outreach programming and hold a community open house in conjunction with this exhibition's opening. The support of this project by the National Endowment for the Arts, a federal agency, is accepted with utmost thanks. The Department of Foreign Affairs and International Trade of Canada also deserves recognition, with special thanks to Yves Pépin and Edythe Good-ridge. Sandra Andel was especially helpful in arranging travel assistance generously provided by American Airlines. The Auxiliary Board of the Art Institute generously funded this exhibition's opening events, and I am especially grateful to co-chairs Will and Ann Hokin as well as Victoria Flanagan. Thanks also go to Susan and Lewis Manilow for graciously hosting the artists during their stay here in Chicago.

"About Place: Recent Art of the Americas" would have been impossible without the initiative and constant support of Director James N. Wood, who demonstrated an unfailing commitment to this ambitious enterprise. I am also grateful to Teri J. Edelstein for her astute administrative instruction, and to Dorothy M. Schroeder for her sage advice and detailed monitoring of this show. Also making important contributions were Robert E. Mars in preparing for Anna Deavere Smith's performance, and Larry Ter Molen for bringing this exhibition to the attention of the Art Institute's Auxiliary Board.

In the course of organizing this exhibition, I have benefited from contributions from fellow curators, scholars, artists, collectors, critics, gallery representatives, and friends. I am particularly indebted to Richard Armstrong for his valuable advice over the entire course of this project, Ann Goldstein for her constant encouragement and her generosity of spirit, and Charles F. Stuckey for his rigorous assessment of my concepts. I received helpful advice from Amada Cruz, Gary Dufour, Richard Francis, Loretta Yarlow, and Lynn Zelevansky regarding the installation. Special thanks go to Sally Wilcox for her assistance with Anna Deavere Smith's performance. Many other friends and colleagues lent an ear, shared ideas, and gave advice and encouragement: sincere thanks to Susanne Ghez, Stephanie Marcus Goodwin, Judith Russi Kirshner, Katy Kline, Susan Lubowsky, Barbara Mirecki, Anne Rorimer, and Rachel Weiss for their wonderful insights. Other individuals gave intellectual advice and support, and I wish to thank Fernando Ayala, Joyce Fernandez, Elizabeth Ferrer, Manuel E. Gonzalez, Kathryn Hixson, Mitchell Kane, Christopher Knight, Lisa Lyons, David Pagel, and Ann Temkin. The enthusiasm and counsel I received from colleagues here has been enormously uplifting:

in particular I wish to thank Judith Barter, Lyn DelliQuadri, Douglas W. Druick, Larry Feinberg, Gloria Groom, Mark Pascale, Martha Tedeschi, Richard Townsend, Ian Wardropper, and Sylvia Wolf for their helpful suggestions and collegiality.

For my travels in Latin America, I relied on the advice of Sandra Antelo-Suarez, Louis Grachos, Gabriel Peluffo, Carolina Ponce de Leon, Mari Carmen Ramírez, Alisa Tager, Jon Tupper, Meyer Vaisman, Ilana Vardy, Clarence and Helena Chapellín Wilson, and Catherine de Zegher. In Latin America I was warmly welcomed by Nora Cohen, Jorge and Marion Helft, Ruth Benzacar, Laura Batkis, and Edward L. Shaw in Buenos Aires; in Montevideo by Alicia Haber; in Santiago by Justo Pastor Mellado; Ivo Mesquita in São Paulo; Paulo Herkenhoff in Rio de Janeiro; and Jairo Valenzuela and Ethel Klenner in Bogota. I owe many thanks to Rina Carvajal and Miguel Miguel in Caracas. In Mexico City I wish to thank Augustín Arteaga of the Museo de Arte Moderno, Magda Carranza of the Centro Cultural/Arte Contemporáneo, and Bertha Cea of the U.S. Embassy. Thanks also go to Maria Guerra, Olivier Debroise, Cuauhtemoc Medina, and especially Kurt Hollander, Rocío Mireles, and Roberto Tejada. In Monterrey I thank Guillermo Sepulveda, Pedro Alonzo, and Ramis Barquet for their assistance.

Of the many who assisted me in my research on Canadian art, I wish to thank Peter Doroshenko, Louis Grachos, David Hartt, and Matthew Teitelbaum. My heartfelt thanks to Richard Rhodes for his advice and welcome to Toronto, where I had the pleasure to meet with Ydessa Hendeles as well as Alan Schwartz, Leontyne Ebers, and Christina Ritchie. In Vancouver I am particularly grateful to Gary Dufour, Keith Wallace, and Scott Watson. In Montreal I wish to acknowledge Regine Basha, René Blouin, Josée Bélisle, Paulette Gagnon, Claude Gosselin, Reesa Greenberg, and Pierre Landry. Diana Nemiroff of the Art Gallery of Ontario was generous with her welcome and advice.

For their expert and gracious assistance in facilitating this exhibition and providing research material on the artists, I am indebted to the following galleries and their staff: David McKee and Bruce Hackney of the David McKee Gallery; Tim Nye; Andrea Rosen and Michelle Reyes of the Andrea Rosen Gallery; Shannon Oksanen on behalf of Rodney Graham; Sean Kelly and Christina Van Schilling of Sean Kelly; Margo Leavin and Steve Henry of the Margo Leavin Gallery; Angela Westwater, David Lieber and Heather White at Sperone Westwater Gallery; Mary Sabbatino and Christine De Metirus of Galerie Lelong; Jack Shainman of the Jack Shainman Gallery; Matthew Marks and Elisabeth Ivers of the Matthew Marks Gallery; Carolyn Alexander, Ted Bonin, and Rhea Anastasi of Brooke Alexander; Charmaine Ferenczi of The Tantleff Office; Olga and Sasha Korper of the Olga Korper Gallery; Phil Smith on behalf of Jeff Wall; and Marian Goodman and Jill Sussman of the Marian Goodman Gallery.

We are enormously grateful to the private collectors and public institutions who have generously shared their much-loved works with us. Their names are acknowledged in the List of Lenders. In addition to those mentioned in the List of Lenders, of crucial assistance in securing works were Dr. Katharina Schmidt of the

Öffentliche Kunstsammlung Basel; Jean-Marc Prevost of the Musée de Rochechouart; Fran Seegull and Bill Begert of The Norton Family Foundation; Sabina Daley of the Bohen Foundation; Dee White of the Anderson Collection; Sharon Essor of Lisson Gallery; and Patrick Painter.

Being relatively new to The Art Institute of Chicago, I am grateful to my more acclimated colleagues for their assistance, good will, and patience. Particular thanks are due to the staff of the Department of Twentieth-Century Painting and Sculpture, especially Courtney Graham Donnell and Daniel Schulman, for offering much-needed advice throughout the project and for relieving me of a myriad of departmental tasks by taking on additional burdens themselves. I am indebted to Kathryn Heston for her steady and calming influence as well as her expert skills, with Barbara Nobares in assistance. Nicholas Barron brought his professional dedication and thoughtful knowledge in art handling to bear on every aspect of this exhibition, ably aided by Richard Holland.

My efforts have been widely and enthusiastically supported at every level of the Art Institute. Thanks to the unflagging efforts of Christine O'Neill, Karin Victoria, Greg Cameron, Greg Perry, and Maria Titterington, as well as Mary Jane Keitel, this project received significant grants. Under the direction of Mary Solt, Darrell Green demonstrated tremendous patience, ingenuity, and good humor while coordinating the loan requests, transport, and insurance of works, which, once on the premises, were ably handled by John Molini and his staff. Under Frank Zuccari's direction, conservators Barbara Hall, Timothy Lennon, and Suzanne Schnepp cared for works of unorthodox material. I am indebted to John Vinci and Alex Krikhaar of the architectural office of John Vinci for a sensitive installation design, and to Calvert Audrain, George Preston, and Ron Pushka for bringing the design to expert fruition. Installation was undertaken under Reynold Bailey's supervision by a superb crew headed by Julio Sims; once complete, it was carefully monitored by Robert Koverman. The exhibition's elegant graphic presentation is due to the efforts of Lyn DelliQuadri and Ann Wassmann.

Fueled by Ronne Hartfield's expert vision, Claire Kunny coordinated the education programs accompanying this exhibition. I thank Luis Camnitzer, Amada Cruz, David Hartt, Susana Torruella Leval, Robert Loescher, Kerry James Marshall, Ivo Mesquita, Diana Nemiroff, and Rachel Weiss for contributing to our educational programming. Thanks are also due to Mary Sue Glosser who, with advice from Neel Keller and especially the generous assistance of Roche Schulfer of the Goodman Theater, facilitated Anna Deavere Smith's performance. Celia Marriott captured this exhibition on videotape. Sincere thanks and appreciation go to Marie Shurkus who, with Carol Becker's endorsement, invited Ann Hamilton and Doris Salcedo to speak at the School of the Art Institute. Eileen Harakal and in particular John Hindman are to be thanked for their public affairs efforts. The unflagging support of these and virtually all other staff members has enabled the success of this project, and I appreciate the help of Jane Clarke, Honore Comfort, Sally-Ann Felgenhauer, Edith Gaines, Nancy Galles, Eileen Gill, Anne Morse, Alexis Petroff, Deborah Schaeffer, Michael Sittenfeld, Leigh Stevenson, and Virginia Voedisch.

The expert assistance of Maureen Lasko and Susan Perry in the Art Institute's Ryerson Library, under the direction of Jack Perry Brown, proved indispensable to my research for the catalogue manuscript. Thanks to interns Lisa Meyerowitz and Viola Michely for their research assistance. The daunting task of producing this catalogue on a short schedule fell upon the Publications Department. Especially challenging was coordinating last-minute revisions endemic to an exhibition of works in progress. To them I owe many thanks for their patience, forebearance, tireless determination, and commitment to this project: Katherine Houck Fredrickson, Robert V. Sharp, Manine Golden, Cris Ligenza, Bryan Miller, and Catherine Steinmann under the supervision of Susan F. Rossen. Terry A. Neff of T. A. Neff Associates skillfully edited this publication. Sam Silvio developed an elegant, sensitive, and original design for this book, enhanced as well by Robert Hashimoto's photography under Alan Newman's supervision. I wish to thank D.A.P./Distributed Art Publishers for distributing this publication.

I am grateful to Dave Hickey and Audrey Weinstein Fosse for enhancing this publication with their scholarly, thoughtful, and original contributions. Curatorial Assistant Audrey Weinstein Fosse has my deep respect and heartfelt thanks for the expert skill she brought to every phase of the exhibition and catalogue and a myriad of curatorial and organizational details. For her extraordinary professionalism, energy, talent, and humor, as well as her unflappable optimism and her unparalleled commitment to this show, I am deeply grateful.

There is no way for me to give adequate thanks to Prudence Carlson, with whom I have enjoyed a decade-long dialogue about art that has profoundly (and happily) influenced my thinking and writing. For her thoughtful intellectual advice and her illuminating insights, not to mention her friendship, I am profoundly thankful. To my husband and companion, Tom Shapiro, I am forever grateful: his perceptive comments on this project, his unfailing and vital encouragement, patience and support have helped this enterprise in every way.

Finally, my deepest gratitude is extended to all the participating artists whose works and ideas initially prompted this project. They have contributed loans from their own collections; they have endured countless telephone calls and interviews; and they have given unstintingly and graciously of their time and assisted me in innumerable other ways. Many of them traveled to Chicago to install new pieces or present earlier ones in thoughtful fresh ways. For their extraordinary efforts, and for the opportunity to be enriched by them and their inspiring art in the process, I am grateful.

Madeleine Grynsztejn
Associate Curator
Twentieth-Century Painting and Sculpture